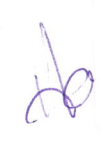

# The Last Roundup

# The Last Roundup

## Stan Graber

Copyright © 1995 by Stan Graber

All rights reserved. No part of this publication may be reproduced, stored in a retrieval system, or transmitted, in any form or by any means, without the prior written permission of the publisher, except in the case of a reviewer, who may quote brief passages in a review to print in a magazine or newspaper, or broadcast on radio or television. In the case of photocopying or other reprographic copying, users must obtain a licence from the Canadian Copyright Licensing Agency • Front cover painting, *Springtime*, by Jim Hauser, reproduced courtesy of the artist • Back cover photograph courtesy Peter Wilson • Cover design by NEXT Communications • Line drawings by Dave Epp, associate designer, *Grainews* • Layout and design by Donald Ward/Ward Fitzgerald editorial design • The publisher gratefully acknowledges the support received from The Canada Council, Heritage Canada, and the Saskatchewan Arts Board.

Printed and bound in Canada by D.W. Friesen & Sons, Altona
95 96 97 98 99/ 5 4 3 2 1

CANADIAN CATALOGUING IN PUBLICATION DATA

Graber, Stan, 1902–
The last roundup
ISBN 1–895618–54–1

1. Graber, Stan, 1902– 2. Cowboys- Saskatchewan-
Biography. 3. Ranch life- Saskatchewan. I. Title.

FC3522.1.G72A3 1995    636.2'0092    C94–920250–9
F1072.G72A3 1995

FIFTH HOUSE LTD.
620 Duchess Street
Saskatoon, SK, Canada S7K 0R1

# Contents

Foreword by Peter Wilson .................................. vi

Preface ............................................................. xi
Acknowledgements ........................................ xiv

## Part One: Wide Open Spaces
At Home on the Range ..................................... 2
Horse Hunting in a Blizzard ............................. 5
On to the Matador ............................................ 9
A Cattle Empire .............................................. 12
The Crows Return .......................................... 17
Old Baldy Gets Frisky .................................... 20

## Part Two: Learning the Ropes
The Night Hawk ............................................. 24
Flying Tails and Kicking Heels ...................... 28
Preparing for the Trail ................................... 33
First Impressions ........................................... 39
The Great Roundup ....................................... 43
Saying Goodbye to a Cowboy ....................... 49

## Part Three: Dusty Trails
Swimming the Saskatchewan ....................... 54
Along the Old Battleford Trail ...................... 59
The Vanishing Crew ...................................... 64
Montana at Last ............................................. 70
Jim Hayes Feels His Oats .............................. 76

## Part Four: So Long
The Comfort of the Coteaus ......................... 82
All in a Day's Work ........................................ 86
Minding the Ranch ........................................ 93
The Old Man Returns .................................... 99
Tough Broncs and Tall Tales ....................... 103
Rustlers on the Range ................................. 106
Hanging Up the Saddle ................................ 110
A Parting Shot ............................................. 116

Cow Country Dictionary ............................. 120

# Foreword

Stan Graber is a writer of remarkable perception and fluency, and a warmhearted human being. Those characteristics emerge in the series of stories that make up his book about prairie life in the first part of the century. The tales are drawn against a backdrop of hard work and wide open spaces, when farmers and ranchers of west central Saskatchewan struggled to build a future for themselves and their families.

Most of the writings were originally published in a popular western Canadian farm paper, *Grainews*, where Stan has been crafting a regular column over the past three years.

His writings, about life on the ranch during the time when cowpunchers were as common on the rural scene as four-wheel-drives are today, provided a good balance with the paper's hard-edged news. Stan's stories of the men and women who made their living with the plough, or a rope and a horse, against a fickle landscape that could take life as quickly as give it, not only brought back memories for old-timers but also painted an accurate historical picture for younger readers.

The funny thing was, Stan never set out in life to be a writer. A cowboy, perhaps, maybe a keen-edged businessman—his careers would incorporate both the saddle and the desk—but becoming a man of words came as somewhat of a surprise. The fact was, however, that his powerful talent for observation, his disarming charm, and a deep curiosity for the world around him meant he was a natural for the job.

What was most surprising was the length of time it took him to finally decide to put pen to paper. He was well into his late eighties before he first signed up to produce what was to become his regular column. Even then it was at the earnest suggestion of the paper's editor; no doubt a newsman with an eye for history as well as increasing circulation.

Stan's columns, focused mainly on his memories of ranching experiences in Saskatchewan in the first twenty years of this century, proved to be a big hit with the paper's readers.

From the obvious wealth of personal experiences, which he draws on to create his stories, it's hard to believe the material he gathered came out of his first two decades of life. A divergent path, taken in his twenties, led him away from the range and into a successful business career.

His business world was to centre around a directorship with Bowman Brothers, a Saskatoon-based wholesale automotive supplier, and later with Gillis and Warren in Winnipeg. While he has fond memories of his business experiences, it's the days when he rode an unfenced prairie that he remembers most vividly. He says he reexperiences those days in his writings.

Now in retirement, and with the loving support of his wife of sixty-five years, Floss, he has finally found the time to relive those early days and share them in his stories.

Stan, even in his ninth decade of life, has no trouble reconnecting with his horse-wrangling days on places like the old Matador Ranch, in west central Saskatchewan. The Colorado-based Matador Land and Cattle Company owned property all over the world: from Saskatchewan Landing to Brazil. As a teenage cowpuncher, Stan was as pleased as punch to be part of the outfit.

There was a great camaraderie among the cowboys, and as a young man the experiences were not lost on Stan, who soaked up the atmosphere like a sponge. Sitting around the campfire or chuck wagon, chewing on sourdough biscuits, beans, and bacon, and listening to tales of cattle rides and rustling gangs that roamed the district was soul food for a young mind.

Stan signed up with the Matador when he was eighteen, riding herd across the rough country of coulees, river flats, and buttes that made up much of the range. Coming from a small-farm background, the sheer size of the territory, and the large herds he had to handle must have posed quite a challenge for the young cowboy. Despite the hardships, Stan remembers those days as a time of deep contentment and happiness.

Now in his early nineties, Stan's days of riding horses and herding prime Hereford beef cattle have long since passed, but his memories of those times are still as sharp as prairie thistle.

Herding, branding, and driving cattle between

pastures were all part and parcel of Stan's job. On one memorable drive, recounted in this book, he helped move more than 3,500 head of cattle south to Montana, fording creeks, streams, and rivers in the process. Incredibly, only one steer was lost during the difficult journey.

Born on a North Dakota ranch, Stan learned to ride at an age when shoelaces were still giving him problems. When his family moved to a Saskatchewan homestead, around 1906, horses continued to play an important role in the young boy's life. As a youngster he'd managed to combine a keen business acumen—a talent that would pay off in later life—with his love of being in the saddle. Hooking up with a telegraph operator in Smiley, a small town northwest of Kindersley, he made a deal to deliver telegrams to the surrounding homesteaders—for a small fee, of course.

It was a heady experience for a young farm lad. This semiprofessional pony-express operation he'd started gave him an opportunity to do what he loved best: ride horses. The part-time job also allowed him to pocket a few dollars a month for his trouble. Stan's eye for a sound business deal began at an early age.

Back then, however, his life was horses, and his small-time entrepreneurial apprenticeship along those dusty prairie trails began on the back of Old Bob. There would be many horses after that, and Stan remembers them all, and their idiosyncrasies.

Some would prove good for night riding, when a sure foot and a steady nerve were needed to brave some of the inky black prairie nights. A horse might be a dab hand at sorting out cattle, making tight turns on the sides of steep slopes, but some of these specialized steeds might get lost as soon as the sun went down.

Hard experience taught Stan about horses. He recalls the time he rode a particular horse that had some kind of kink in the right side of its neck. Stan figures that kink must have had a connection with the moon's gravitational pull, or maybe magnetic north, because given half the chance that's the direction the horse would always turn.

Stan remembers the names of the horses almost as well as the cowpunchers who rode them. Horses and Stan were inseparable, that was until a day in his early twenties, when he exchanged his saddle for a desk and his lariat for a pen and began his business career in a small bank in Elrose.

No doubt, recalling in Technicolored reality the events of youth is the rich comfort that old age gradu-

*Three old-time cattlemen reminisce about the good old days on the open range before the advance of the plough. (l–r) Pete Perrin, Jesse Perrin, Stan Graber, 1994.* Courtesy Peter Wilson of *The StarPhoenix*

ally hands to lucky ones among us. But Stan relies on his excellent memory to supply the detail and provide the colour and texture of life in those early days. He never allows himself to dip into a well of sentimental nostalgia that can become the quicksand for even the most seasoned reporter's reminiscences.

Looking back on the change in lifestyle he chose more than seventy years ago, Stan says he has no regrets. The road that took him into the business world brought him much satisfaction and success. He does, however, wonder what might have happened if he'd stayed riding the range.

Peter Wilson

*This scene is deep in the heart of "Matador country" and can be reached on a graded trail from either Kyle, on the west, or Beechy, on the east. Visitors are greeted by deer running in the deep coulees, and by golden eagles and falcons, which nest in the high cliffs. Lake Diefenbaker is visible in the background.* **Courtesy Peter Wilson of** *The StarPhoenix*

# Preface

I was fifteen years old when my family took up ranching near the town of Elrose, Saskatchewan, in 1917. In addition to owning the ranch, my father worked as an elevator agent and also ran the local butcher shop. We lived in town, and used the ranch for holding and grazing the livestock Father bought and sold. Often steer stockers were purchased in the spring, held on grass all summer, then shipped by rail to the Winnipeg market. Beef was held on pasture and slaughtered as needed for the shop in Elrose.

Grazing fees for horses, taken for the summer, were sufficient to pay most of the operating expenses for the ranch. We also received a few dollars for grazing cows and calves brought to us by farmers. We never gathered cattle, nor returned them, as they were too troublesome and slow on the trail. Nor did we hold stock from one year to the next. The ranch closed at the end of October and did not reopen until the snow had disappeared the following spring.

Although I, along with our hired man, spent many long days and nights amid the rolling hills and sheltered coulees of our ranch, we saw no need to erect any buildings there. An eight-by-ten-foot tent, hidden in a deep gully and protected from the wind, served as home. It was here that I slept and cooked, and ate my meals. And it was here as I lay listening to the coyotes call and the wind shuffle through the virgin grassland that I dreamt of a life in the saddle and working for one of the big outfits that were so prominent in the area at that time.

For a short time those dreams became reality. When I was eighteen, I was given the opportunity of a lifetime when I rode as a cowpuncher for the Canadian division of the Matador Land and Cattle Company Limited. The Matador was the largest ranching empire in the world. Its Canadian range, assembled in 1903, was a spread of 140,000 acres in the Coteau Hills, north of the Saskatchewan River. From its large breeding ranches in Texas and Oklahoma, the Matador company shipped young cattle to the northern states of South Dakota and Montana, and to its Swift

Current ranch in Saskatchewan, Canada, to mature and fatten. In this way the company raised and marketed thousands of prime beef cattle, and made substantial yearly profits.

In 1920 and 1921, I learnt what it meant to "ride the range" as I drove herds of beef cattle to the shipping pens at Wiseton, Saskatchewan, and night-herded horses in the quiet of a prairie evening. I also participated in the final roundup of stock that occurred when the Matador closed the books on its Canadian operation and 3,500 bawling cattle were driven 350 miles from the Canadian Matador to the Montana ranch on the Milk River, at Harlem, Montana. It was the last of the long cattle drives. Farming and settlement were replacing the open range, and the face of the frontier would never be the same.

I worked with people (and horses) who are seldom far from my thoughts, even though most of them are long gone and more than seventy years have passed. The Canadian manager of the Matador, J.R. Lair, known affectionately as the "Old Man" or "Legs," stood six foot six in his socks and was as honest as he was tall. Legs and his wagon foreman, Cy Thornton, were Texans. Handsome Jimmy Reynolds, the top hand, was from Oklahoma, and proved to me that friendship was measured in actions not words. Quiet, honest Archie Hawes rode the rough string, breaking broncs, and could preach a tolerable sermon on Sunday. Jim Hayes, an eccentric and shell-shocked World War I veteran of English-Eurasian parentage, was the wagon cook. His mastery of a sourdough crock was acknowledged as the best by ranchers throughout the Coteau Hills. Crusty and cantankerous, or soft spoken and thoughtful, I admired and learned something from each of these honest, skilled cattlemen.

A cowboy is nothing without his horse, and the Saskatchewan Matador and its riders had a remuda of 125 good mounts. Most of these horses were trained and ridden for specific jobs in working cattle. There were cutting, roping, and circle horses, as well as sure-footed night horses. Among the best of these were Bootjack, Black Bird, White Man, Silver, Creepy, Star, and good old homely Buck, who could do a good job no matter what was asked of him.

It is my intention to capture the spirit of those days in my writing: to paint a picture of a riding ranch-hand at work and to allow the reader to relive the last days of the Canadian Matador through the eyes of a young man who fancied himself a cowboy.

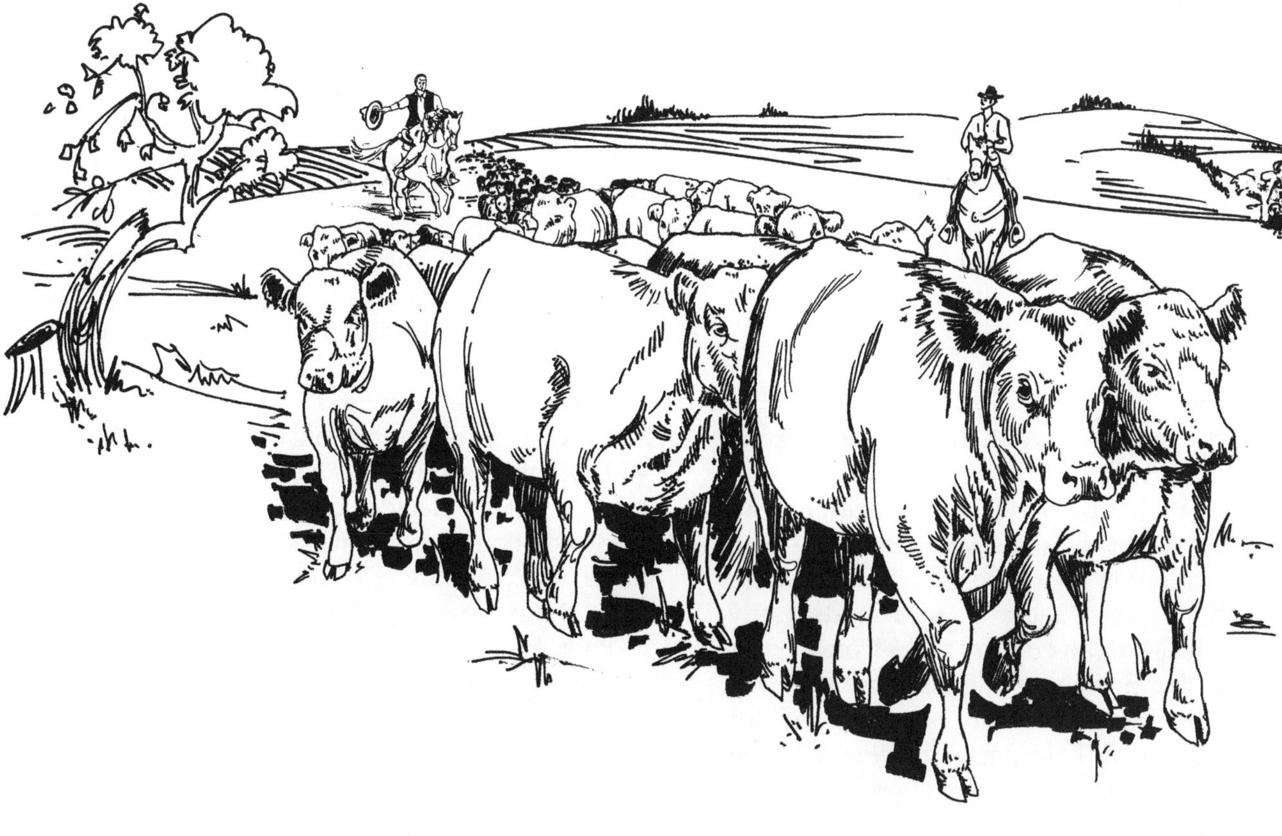

# Acknowledgements

There are many people I owe thanks for helping me put this book together.

Thomas R. Smith provided old Saskatchewan ranch maps and old brand registration books, as well as information about many of the old ranches. Walter and Marj McCrie drove me and my friends many miles through the Matador country of the Coteau Hills to refresh my memory about the geography of this grand old ranch. I thank these nice people as well for the deep sleeps and full stomachs that Perry Olson and I were treated to when we were overnight guests in the McCrie home.

To each member of the Perrin family—from the oldest to the youngest—I owe my appreciation for help in composing this book. Many of the pictures herein are from their files. For this, and your friendship, thank you very much.

I am grateful to Carol and Thomas Inocencio (Cliff Beech's daughter and her husband, who live in Banning, California) for lending me the pictures that have become a part of *The Last Roundup*. Your presence brings Cliff's spirit back. It is almost as if the two of us were once again riding in a pasture where there is always good water and tall grass.

It was wonderful to find Opal Bradford in Texas, a sister to Cy (Tom) Thornton, our old wagon boss. Thanks, Opal, for trusting us with your irreplaceable photographs of the American Matador crews and for the biographical information about Tom and your family. I am also obliged to Larry Lefler, who rode for the Matador in 1919 and 1920, for providing Opal's address.

Peter Wilson has allowed his photographs to appear here and was kind enough to prepare a foreword. He is a fine man and a good friend.

Colin Grant and the staff at Luther Heights were very supportive and showed unflagging interest in the book. I am grateful for the use of their office equipment as I prepared the manuscript. I thank them, too, for their help in winning many battles with an ornery computer.

Perry Olson, a true and loyal friend, was always there when I sought honest criticism. It was grand to follow in his shadow at the branding roundup, where he showed his great skill as a heel roper.

Keith Berglind, associate editor at *Grainews*, was the person who encouraged me to write in the first place. He also arranged for the line drawings and the maps that appear here. His enthusiasm has made this book possible.

Dave Epp, associate designer at *Grainews*, is responsible for the fine line drawings that appear throughout the book.

Charlene Dobmeier, my editor, is a gentle lady of great patience who has become a good friend during the year that we have worked together on this book.

To all of you, my deepest thanks.

To Floss, with love

# Part One
# Wide Open Spaces

# At Home On the Range

The large, heavy page-wire corral was already in the south fork of Twin Coulee when my family took over the lease on our ranch, located six miles south and west of Elrose in southern Saskatchewan. There was a sturdy drift fence commencing at the gate and running out from the southwest corner, and high shoulders, to your right and left, as you rode toward the narrow entrance of the coulee. Directly in front of the rider, as he rode southeast, was a ridge that separated the coulee into the north and south forks. No one seems to know who built the corral. Some assume that the cattle-rustling Jennings family had chosen the coulee because it was so well hidden. Two riders, on good horses, could funnel two or three hundred head of stock into the corral with hardly a sound.

The large, well-worn snubbing post in the middle of the corral, and the depth of manure, would indicate a great many cattle had gone into, and out of, this old structure. How many cattle? How long ago? Only the ghost of an old Indian, buried on the pinnacle high above the corral, would have the answers.

Compared with most ranches in the area, the Graber ranch was small, less than three thousand acres. It was bound on the west by the eastern shores of White Bear Lake. The butte, behind our camp and corrals, to the northeast, was so high that I never walked or rode a horse to its top.

At the northwest corner of our pasture, the fence ran south about three-quarters of a mile, to White Bear Lake. To the north, farm fences already covered most of the way, so we had only to string a few miles of barbed wire to snugly enclose our lease of rolling hills and sheltered coulees.

In several of the larger coulees there were bubbling springs of clear, cool water that fed small creeks, which ran into the lake. The largest of these springs was encircled by a half-acre bog of blue quicksand.

There were many mornings when I had to use my saddle horse to pull out a big cow that had become trapped in the bog. The strongest and best horse that I had for this job was Jess, a big blue roan mare.

Our ranch camp was quite high on the sloping walls of the north fork. The tent and camping grounds—backed into a quiet, flat spot—escaped the strong winds that swept up and down the coulee. Our furnishings consisted of a sheet-metal cook stove that burned buffalo chips. It had a good-sized fire box and an oven for baking. The stove was collapsible and could be carried on a pack horse. An old apple box served as a cupboard.

The fanciest piece of furniture was the single bed. We had salvaged a panel door left behind on the prairie by some homesteader when he abandoned his shack. We drove six willow pickets into the ground and placed the door on them. This served as our bunk under the stars for the next couple of years.

The prairie night provided some curious bedfellows. There were bees, wasps, and ants. One night, just before falling asleep, I felt something on the fold

*Fifteen-year-old Stan beside the tent he called "home" on the Graber ranch, deep in the White Bear Hills.* Author Photo

# 4 The Last Roundup

in the blanket at my chin. It was a fat prairie mouse sitting on my chest, scratching his ear.

Coyotes sang. We were surrounded by a chorus of their voices. A clear, lyric soprano was at our doorstep. A deep bass responded high up the butte at our back. There were altos and tenors on every hill where the moon was shining.

Skunks called on us, as did porcupines and timid jack rabbits. There were visits by weasels, badgers, and other members of this family. Once, the largest and most dangerous of them, a wolverine, came to call. Of course, all around us were gophers, some with stripes; there were busy chipmunks, always mice, flies, and mosquitoes.

By the light of a coal oil lantern, we read Ainsworth and Irving, and when the little English magazine came in, "The Boys Lost in the Florida Everglades." We were never lonely.

Awakening to the song of a meadowlark and the chirping of a sparrow, one knew it would be a good day.

*Cliff Beech* (left), *scratching and fanning Old Devil to a standstill. This picture was taken at a Sunday rodeo at the Graber ranch in July 1918. Although he broke hundreds of tough, wild horses, Cliff was never thrown from the saddle.*
Courtesy Mr. and Mrs. Thomas Inocencio

# Horse Hunting In a Blizzard

Weather in late March 1918 was warm, overcast, calm, and sort of depressing. The snow had disappeared by 1 April in all but the deepest coulees. It had grown so warm that we were tempted to pack away our heavy winter clothing.

Our hired hand, Cliff Beech, and I thought it was about time to round up the horses that had been wintering out in the White Bear Hills—at least that's where we thought they were. So, on 2 April, we saddled up and rode south and west of Elrose for six or eight miles, near our ranch. There had been a nice spell of weather for quite some time, so riding was very comfortable. You could see for miles. It felt good to get out after being confined all winter.

Cliff was a great companion and friend. He was a tall man, slim, good looking, and easy going. Each spring he was occupied breaking broncs into good saddle horses. Then, in the summer, when the towns had their sports days and exhibitions, he had a string of running horses that usually made him pretty good money. One of his successes was Kangaroo, a big red thoroughbred imported from eastern Canada that Cliff had tamed and turned into a fine race horse.

As we rode through the White Bear Hills, heading south, we saw no sign of our horses. Even from the south rim overlooking the Sanctuary Flats, where we could see for miles, we were greeted by an apparently empty prairie. It was getting late, so we decided to ride to the Jack Horne farm and ranch a few miles farther south where we knew we could stay the night.

Jack Horne and his brother Ernie were early settlers in this area on the east shore of White Bear Lake. Jack was an excellent housekeeper and cook. He was, by profession, a baker, and he always set a good table. He enjoyed visitors and expressed his pleasure in strong, salty language, except in the presence of ladies, of course. When I met him twenty years later, he hadn't changed a bit. He greeted me with hugs and expressions of endearment that questioned my parentage and my chances of making it to heaven.

Jack raised prize-winning Percheron horses, and among his saddle horses was the most beautiful, small, almost white, dapple grey Arabian mare. She was, of course, small boned but strong for her size, as most Arabians are. Her head was perfect, with the usual Arabian-dished face. She had dark eyes and nostrils, giving her a very intelligent appearance. I remember watching Jack ride across the prairies in deep snow. Even with his heavy riding equipment, she carried him easily at a slow and gentle canter.

As always, Jack was pleased to see us. After supper, we retired early. Cliff and I made a bed on the living room floor with a few blankets. Jack and Ernie slept in single bunks in the corner of the living room.

We fell asleep quickly; it had been a long day in the saddle. About two hours later I awoke with a queer feeling and a terrible throbbing in my head. I must have been lying on my back, which was fortunate, for when I opened my eyes I noticed shadows of flame dancing across the ceiling. My first thought was fire, and I got up as quickly as I could in my befuddled condition. I threw open the outside door and then stumbled to the kitchen range where I discovered that, before going to bed, Jack had filled the stove with coal and left the stove lid partially open. Coal gas and smoke were now going directly into the house rather than up the chimney.

I managed to wake everyone and had them get up and move around to be sure they were all right. After the house was aired out, we all went back to bed, but there was little chance of sleeping due to our throbbing heads.

Had I not awakened, we would surely have died.

After taking care of the horses in the morning, we had a big breakfast of bacon and eggs, and lots of Jack's good toast with Wagstaffe jam and great mugs of steaming coffee.

We had decided by now that our horses must have been led back to the Coteau Hills by a couple of Cliff's horses that came from that great range country. Most likely they had wintered there. After breakfast, we rode directly to the High Point area. High Point—elevation 2,850 feet—was, as its name suggests, the highest point of land in the Coteau Hills. For years there was a post office there, serving the ranchers in the area, and run by Mr. and Mrs.

Haltam, an English couple who settled there in the pioneer years. Mr. Haltam hauled the mail by horse team from Elrose once a week, winter and summer, rain or shine.

From High Point, we rode south ten miles or so, almost to Clearwater Lake, then east several miles and then back north. When we finally found the horses, it was getting late, and we knew we would have to find some place to spend the night. We decided to head for the Les Giauque ranch, some distance from where we were.

The wind, from the northwest, had been increasing in velocity all day. It turned to sleet, then snow. Soon we were in the midst of a blizzard.

The dog announced our arrival at the Giauque ranch, and Les came to the door and shouted to us

*Cliff Beech* (right) *and his brother, Ray, breaking broncs. The horse Cliff is astride was called Vegule, and developed into a speedy race horse.*
Author Photo

to put the horse herd in the corral and the saddle horses in the barn.

Les did not know yet who his visitors were, but in those years that did not matter. He would find out after we had taken care of our horses and he had welcomed us into his home. He gave us a hand feeding and watering the horses, and, once inside, Mrs. Giauque made us feel welcome by putting on a couple of extra plates for supper.

Cliff and I had had nothing to eat all day, and after our long, cold ride, we were ravenous. I know we ate too much, which accounted, no doubt, for my feeling ill that night.

The Giauques raised mostly horses on their ranch. These were the days before tractors, and there was a lot of demand for the animals. However, a large and growing family meant that expenses were often higher than the ranch's income.

In order to meet this challenge, Les ran stampedes—now known as rodeos—and he rented out bucking horses to others who ran stampedes. He was a fabulous bronc rider—a small man but incredibly strong. He awed his audiences with tricks such as grasping the saddle horn and throwing himself from one side of a fast-running horse to the other, touching the ground on each side of the horse as he threw himself back and forth.

Cliff and I made our bed in the middle of the small living room on the floor under the dining room table, very near the kitchen range. We felt fortunate to have such shelter as we listened to the blizzard rage outside.

I fell asleep quickly but had not been dozing long when I was awakened with stomach cramps. Storm or no storm, I hurried into my boots, jammed on my hat, and headed for the outside biffy, clad only in my long johns. I made many visits to the great outdoors that night, and Cliff became quite annoyed with me for inadvertently spilling a good deal of snow on him as I climbed back into bed after yet another visit.

Morning eventually arrived, and, in those days, there was no excuse for illness. We started out for Elrose, which lay about thirty-five miles to the northwest.

We had a fifteen-to-eighteen-horse herd, and, as some of them were pretty wild, we decided to "tail" them. This was done by taking a lead rope from one horse and attaching it to the tail of the next horse, and so forth. We divided the horses into two strings of eight or nine. Cliff took the lead rope and I brought up the tail end, or "drag." In this fashion, we headed directly into the howling wind.

# On to The Matador

We rode into the wind all day, without suitable clothing or covering, especially over our faces. After what seemed an eternity, we decided to go to the John Campbell farm, located a few miles from Elrose. The Campbells were distantly related by marriage to Cliff, and we knew we could get feed and shelter for our horses, and a haven for ourselves.

We arrived at the Campbells' just after dark, put the horses in the corral, and threw them some oat bundles. When we got into the house, we almost collapsed. We had not realized how close to exhaustion we were.

Mrs. Campbell knew exactly how to treat our wind- and cold-burned faces. She put thick cow's cream, almost like butter, on our burns and blisters. But she could do little for our heads, which were still throbbing from the coal gas episode at Jack Horne's.

Those two days of horse hunting in a blizzard were probably two of the longest days in my life. I will never forget the hospitality of those wonderful pioneer people who, without question, opened their homes and provided food they could ill afford to spare. They would have been deeply offended had we offered to pay them. Their reward was knowing they had done for us what we would have done for them.

Our family butcher shop had not been profitable for some time, so Dad sold it in the spring of 1920. Our ranch, however, did not go with the deal, as it was an ideal holding place for the cattle that Father bought for the Winnipeg market.

Early spring of 1920 found Cliff Beech riding with us again. There were cows and their calves grazing on the new green prairie wool. This grass, of fescue and blue stem, was so rich in nutrients that the calves appeared to grow taller right before your eyes. You could hear the cows growing fatter. Optimism was in the air. It was spring.

For Cliff and me, it was a busy time of year. Miles of fence had to be ridden and broken spots fixed. Saddles and ranch equipment needed mending, and

## 10 The Last Roundup

winter hair in the coats, manes, and tails of the saddle stock had to be combed. There was no time for idleness.

It must have been the moccasin telegraph that carried the message that the Matador Ranch was short of experienced riders. Even though we were busy on the ranch, Dad and Cliff could see the excitement this news brought me. To a youngster, the idea of qualifying for a job riding for this mysterious Texas outfit was a dream come true. I headed out for the Matador that same day.

I caught the Matador wagon crew near Bootjack Tank (a dammed-up spring and watering place) on its way home for the night. The men saw me coming and slowed slightly until I rode along beside them.

*Cliff Beech* (right) *and his helpers at the Graber ranch at roundup time. Note the ten-gallon milk can on the stoneboat. This was used to haul drinking water from Onemile Spring. Judging from the "fancy" attire of the man in the middle, it was a Sunday.*
Courtesy Mr. and Mrs. Thomas Inocencio

There were no greetings of any sort. No questions were asked; they were not necessary. The men had other ways of judging an unfamiliar rider.

They could tell from the salt of the dried sweat on Baldy's shoulders that we had ridden long and hard miles that day. They could see from the way I sat my horse, the shiny leather on my saddle, and my worn chaps that I was an experienced rider for one so young. They did not ask my name, or where I had come from, or where I was going. The unwritten code of the early West said that those were questions not asked of a stranger.

Jim Hayes, the chuck-wagon cook, and Cy (Tom) Thornton, the wagon boss, made me welcome. After a good supper and a smoke, we sat comfortably on bedrolls in the big tent. The silence was broken abruptly by snorting horses and the tinkling of bells; it was the "jingle hour" of dusk. This is when the horse wrangler drives the remuda into the rope corral so that a change of horses can be made. It is also the time for the night hawk to begin herding the saddle stock until jingle time, at day break, next morning.

I was in awe of my new surroundings, and the men of the Matador. Never before had I seen such beautiful saddle horses, in one group, as were in the Matador remuda. They were all geldings; ladies were excluded.

Gathering my courage, I told Cy Thornton that local rancher Lawrence Ohmacht had sent word to me that the Matador was looking for an experienced cowhand, and that I had come seeking the job. Cy hired me. That very night I stood guard on the horse herd. My first job at the Matador was night-hawking the remuda.

I had started work at the Matador just after the spring shipments of young steers had arrived, by train, in 1920. The stock came from one of the breeding ranches in Texas up to the Wiseton shipping pens, one mile east of this new town on the Elrose branch of the Canadian National Railway. The pens were forty miles north of the Matador. Already the cattle were grazing in the north summer pasture.

I worked out of Bootjack camp. From here the Matador cowhands checked and repaired all of the fences enclosing the northwest corner of their lease. There were sand hills in this area, and for some reason, fence posts dry rot sooner here than in heavy clay. All of these rotted posts had to be replaced. It took two or three weeks, with a slip scraper and a walking plough, to move the earth and repair the watering hole at Laidly Springs, to the far west, and on the dam at Bootjack Tank.

While most of the cowhands were busy riding, and repairing fences, and doing the hard work of moving earth, the night hawk slept during the day and wrangled the saddle stock during the long night hours. His was an easier job, but lonely.

The four-strand barbed wire fence surrounding the north summer pasture ran a total of forty-eight miles. It took the better part of the summer before we put the last new post in the ground on the eastern end of this eighteen-mile-long enclosure.

After this came the roundup; time to gather the cattle and run them through the "dip-vat." This was a treatment for the eradication of mange. Rounding up great herds of cattle is always exciting, and so it was in 1920. It took three days of hard riding before Thornton's wagon crew had eight thousand head of steers grazing in the dip-vat pasture.

Winter came early in 1920, catching the chuck wagon breaking trail through snow on its way to Wiseton with 2,500 head of beef to ship to Great Britain.

# A Cattle Empire

The Matador Land and Cattle Company Limited was incorporated in 1882 when a syndicate of Scottish commercial bankers created what was to become the largest and most successful empire devoted solely to raising beef cattle. These careful Scots invested recklessly in the 1880s in both North and South America. One of their greatest adventures in creating the Matador was securing a lease on 1,500,000 acres on the upper Pease River in western Texas.

Another achievement of these canny Scots was to engage one of the best cattlemen in the world, Murdo Mackenzie, as their North American manager, a man Theodore Roosevelt referred to as "the most influential of western cattlemen." Mackenzie was a Scottish, university-educated investment banker with a background in raising cattle. He already had practical experience in managing the Prairie Cattle Company

Limited, situated in southeastern Colorado and adjacent territories.

The policy of the Matador directors in Scotland to use the yearly profits for expansion rather than for the payment of dividends for the first years enabled the company to expand into larger holdings in Wyoming, Montana, South Dakota, Nebraska, Oklahoma, New Mexico, Saskatchewan, and larger areas of Texas. An affiliated company in Brazil, at one time managed by Mackenzie, had large holdings in cattle, land, and even six thousand miles of railroads on its vast properties.

A major factor in Mackenzie's successful management was his policy of continually improving the quality of the cattle by importing onto the Matador's breeding ranges thousands of the best Hereford bulls that Great Britain could supply.

He also had the faculty of successfully managing people—especially those independent American cattlemen who resented outside interference or change. He led by example and hard work. He was a wise man who persuaded the cattlemen to work with the marketing boards and the railroads. Previously these groups had been adversaries, and now, by negotiation, there were benefits for all. Mackenzie was a man of vision, always fair and strictly honest.

By 1900, Matador officials, and especially Mackenzie, realized that raising great herds of cattle, on even their empirelike southern ranges, created grazing problems. Then came the dry years of 1901 and 1902 causing overgrazing, especially near permanent springs, dams, and watering holes. A partial solution to this was to drill deep wells and install windmills, pumps, and tanks where grass was still good in the distant parts of the range.

Experience proved that cattle that were trail-driven or later shipped by rail to the northern, cooler ranges as young stock, finished 150 pounds heavier than they would have had they matured on southern grass. As well, they brought a higher market price, especially in Chicago.

Apparently, Mackenzie was advised that the Canadian government was not adverse to leasing large tracts of good grazing prairie land in what is now the province of Alberta. In July of 1903, Mackenzie arrived in Medicine Hat to search for available land in the Land Titles Office.

While there he met his old friend Horseshoe Smith (Henry Smith). The two journeyed to Lethbridge and Calgary. They soon found that the southern Alberta country, within the mild chinook wind area, with its snow-melting tendencies, was already too settled by homesteaders and small ranchers to make a large ranch practical. However, they learned of an area on the north side of the Saskatchewan river, about twenty-five miles north of the station of Swift Current in what would become the province of Saskatchewan.

Mackenzie was so impressed with the reports about the Saskatchewan land that he left for Swift Current at once. There he hired a democrat wagon (a buckboard) and a camping outfit, including tents and mosquito netting, good horses, and a driver, to take him to the Saskatchewan Landing on the river where the government had established a ferry. He was told in Swift Current that at the Landing settlement there

*Legs Lair* (far left), *manager of the Canadian Matador, and Murdo Mackenzie* (second from left) *on the Saskatchewan Landing ferry, circa 1912. The man on the right is the ferry-man.*
**Courtesy the Perrin Family**

lived a reliable old Metis by the name of Isidore Laplante, who could guide him through the immense area on the north side of the river. This rolling prairie land included the Coteau Hills, east and north of the Landing, the White Bear Hills, forty miles north and west, and Bone Pile Ridge, almost directly west.

Little is known about Isidore Laplante. One can assume, and probably quite accurately, that he was born in Manitoba of French-Canadian Metis parents. It appears that he married there while quite young, and by this first marriage had several children. He moved to the Landing on the Saskatchewan River from Manitoba in the late 1890s, bringing with him his two youngest sons, Pete and Isidore Jr. Reliable records show that Isidore's second marriage was to Felaime Trochey, a Saskatchewan-born Metis woman. They were married in Swift Current in 1909. At the time, Felaime would have been twenty years of age and Isidore sixty-seven. Other records indicate that Felaime was possibly eighteen and Isidore sixty-eight—a difference of about fifty years. By 1921, Isidore and Felaime had nine living children.

Isidore Laplante was a large man, six feet tall, heavy boned, wide of shoulders, and very strong. A dignified manner and large physical appearance at once created a favourable impression. He was a fine boatman and, in years to come, always assisted the Matador men when they were swimming cattle across the Saskatchewan River.

His two grown sons, Pete and Isidore, Jr., were giants, much taller and heavier than their father. They, too, were good with oars in fast-running water. They were of good character and willing workers. Neither of them married, and they lived for years in the Coteau Hills, trapping and ranching, and occasionally working for the Perrin boys when these fine ranchers ran the Matador community pasture after about 1923.

In July of 1903, when Mackenzie first met Isidore Laplante, he knew that he was indeed fortunate in finding this man to guide him. First he had Laplante check the outfit he had hired in Swift Current. Isidore approved but added a couple of saddle horses and riding equipment for use in the rougher parts of the country they would be exploring.

Both Mackenzie and Laplante were men of few words, and neither wasted time in small talk. Their backgrounds were worlds apart: Mackenzie was a university-educated, commercial banker and cattleman; Laplante, who lacked formal education, had a natural, quiet dignity that enhanced his wisdom and intelligence. At this time, he was sixty-one, and Mackenzie was fifty-three years old. The two men quickly grew to respect one another.

As the small caravan journeyed over the endless miles of virgin prairie, the men noted the deep carpet of blue stem and grama grass. Mackenzie, in his report to Scotland, later said: "The grass covered every inch of the ground and to the top of the mountains." He noted good water everywhere and this, along with large canyonlike coulees along the north side of the Saskatchewan River for winter shelter, would make a good place for a large cattle ranch.

He thought the most desirable land to rent would be the six townships to the east and north of the Saskatchewan Landing. The southwest corner of the first township would be about four miles east of the Landing. From there, the area selected would go about twelve miles north and eighteen miles east. This area of six townships would encompass 216 sections of 640 acres each, or a total of 138,240 acres. Ike Blasingame, in writing about the days he rode for the Canadian Matador in 1905, said that, in addition to this immense piece of rangeland, Matador cattle grazed to as far as seventy miles north of the Saskatchewan River on open range. This would mean that in the early years Matador cattle grazed as far north as the present-day towns of Rosetown, Milden, and Conquest.

Mackenzie recommended to Scotland that they start negotiating at once for a twenty-one-year lease with the Canadian government. The lease he proposed would exclude from the area all farmers and small ranchers, thus giving the Matador complete control over the area rented and saving them from possible litigation involving right of entry and other possible areas of disagreement.

He proposed, too, that the lease provide for a reasonable number of years' notice of cancellation by either party, and that there be no penalty if so cancelled.

At this time an unusual and fortunate situation developed: Mr. Alexander Mackay, secretary of the Matador board in Scotland, was on his annual inspection trip to their North American holdings. On this trip Mackay planned a short visit with his brother-in-law, W.A. Burns, in Ottawa. Mr. Burns was manager of the Bank of Nova Scotia in Ottawa and also a personal friend of the land commissioner.

It appears that the negotiation for a long-term lease on the desired Saskatchewan land was quickly agreed to by the Matador and the Canadian Land Department. Thus began one of the largest cattle ranches in Canada.

# The Crows Return

Winter came all too soon in 1920. That summer and fall we were so busy at the Matador that mid-November was upon us before we realized it. The north summer pasture (six miles north and south by eighteen miles east and west) had been cleared entirely of all stock, horses too. All eight thousand or so head had been brought south to the dip-vat pasture on the river. The fall roundup had been completed and the beef trail-herded north to our shipping pens on the CN railway just east of Wiseton.

I awoke in the bunkhouse at the Matador headquarters one morning and realized that my first season at the ranch had slipped by. It was time to pack my "war bag" and bedroll for the ride home to Elrose, about forty-five or fifty miles northwest. Old Baldy, my sturdy little horse, was at the hitching rail at the door, already saddled, and, as usual, anxious to get on the trail.

The manager of the ranch, Mr. Lair, sent Scotty Reid, the secretary, out to ask me to come into his office before I left. As well as saying goodbye, Mr. Lair wanted to be sure I knew he wanted me back in the spring of 1921 to ride for them again. I promised to return and we shook hands. We agreed I would be back next spring, just before the crows returned.

My father and I had a pack of wolf hounds, and every day that the snow was right I hunted coyotes. I had a very successful winter hunting season. I don't remember exactly how many coyotes I caught—likely thirty or more. The price for hides was very good, too, so it helped the family coffers in those not-too-prosperous years.

Spring surprised us by arriving early that year. The snow disappeared quickly, and the crows began to arrive. It was time for me to report for work at the Matador for my second season. Mother had washed all the blankets in my bedroll. The standard bedroll for riding ranch-hands in those years was two full-sized "soogans," at least two full-sized heavy woollen blankets, and a feather pillow. While at the Matador, I was given a very special woollen blanket from the First World War, which was perfect for a bedroll. This blanket and a colourful Navaho saddle blanket are the only relics I have left from my cowpunching days.

Soogan was, I believe, a Scottish name for a down-filled comforter bed throw. Anyway, these lightweight blankets were folded double, lengthwise, one on top of the other, and made a soft and warm mattress. There were no cotton sheets.

The blankets and the soogans were placed in the

*A night hawk captures a bit of shuteye after herding the remuda from dusk to dawn. Notice the bedroll, the cowboy's "sleeping bag." The photo was taken in Montana in the 1890s.*
Courtesy Glenbow-Alberta Institute/NA–207–113

centre of a canvas tarp, sixteen by eighteen feet. Half the length of the tarp was on the bottom and half on the top. The two sides of the tarp were now folded over the top; one side had rings and the other side had snaps. The head part was now folded back and the pillow put in place.

There was now about two feet of the tarp left by the pillow. This space was used for your war bag, which contained personal items such as a razor, shaving kit, and so on, and maybe a few extra clothes.

The head of the tarp was now folded in, and then the bed was rolled up from the head to the foot. There were two leather straps or two small ropes, and these were used to tie the bedroll into a neat bundle that could be thrown around without coming apart. This bed, if properly made, would stay that way for a week or ten days even if tossed about on a pack horse or behind the cantle on your saddle.

There were many types of horses necessary in ranching. Some were bred purposely for one type of work or another. Some seemed to take more easily to becoming good cutting horses—the most prized—or others good roping horses, or gentle and sure-footed night horses.

Then there were those high-strung, sure-footed, speedy little broncs that could run for miles and hours without tiring. These probably were the most exciting of all. They were called "circle horses" and were used for rounding up cattle on big ranges. My little Baldy was such a horse. He was a bay. The right side of his head was all white, and from this, he looked out of a "glass eye" that never missed a gopher hole. In all the years that I rode this sturdy little horse, he never fell with me—not even in the inky black of a prairie night. I talked with him on many long and lonely rides and I know that he understood, for there was always a sharp gleam of comprehension in his glass eye.

Baldy was grain fed and hard from winter riding. His small and nicely formed hooves were shod all around, and after a mile or two of warming up, he started on his own with his fast, ground-eating lope. He would usually lead with his right front foot, but on occasion would switch to a left-foot lead.

Your seat never left the saddle, and the perpetual rolling tended to lull one to sleep. At these times, the prairie wool of carpet came and was gone. Only when a nearby meadowlark sang, or a surprised coyote came out of the low buck brush, was our rhythmic flow interrupted.

As always, when spring arrived my lively imagination went into overdrive. I dreamt of being the owner of a big outfit with a great prairie full of white-faced cattle. I would have the best of ranch-hands and the most benevolent foreman.

My dreaming was interrupted as we went by the west shore of Clearwater Lake and to the west of Lawrence Ohmacht's ranch. Then we arrived at the gate, about four miles east of the northwest corner of the Matador summer pasture. I know of no one who ever used this gate except me. We were now about fifteen or so miles from the Matador headquarters on the South Saskatchewan River.

On arrival at the ranch, about 4:30 in the afternoon, we were greeted warmly by Mr. Lair and the foreman, Cy Thornton. It was wonderful to be back with working friends of a year ago, and I looked forward to another season on the Matador.

# Old Baldy Gets Frisky

When it was Baldy's turn to be ridden, I staked him to my saddle on good grass. This spot was forty or fifty yards below our camp. The old boy was well rope broke, so I never dreamed he would pull the stunt he did.

While fixing breakfast at our camp in the big coulee on the Graber ranch, I peeked out of the tent and saw great bundles of tumbleweed rolling up the coulee past Baldy. The old horse had his back to the cold, hard-driving northwest wind as tumbleweed flew by him on all sides. At the very moment I was watching, a small band of wild horses ran from the hills above and down into the coulee. They flashed past Baldy and vanished into the haze of the White Bear Valley.

In an instant, my only means of transportation disappeared to the northwest in a cloud of dust. I was afoot! To an old cowpuncher, nothing could be worse. To a young one, it brought tears.

Regaining my composure, and after a couple of hard snorts on my handkerchief, I started to walk in the general direction my former friend had taken. I found Old Baldy soaking my saddle in the muddy end of White Bear Lake. He had dragged my pride and joy—the best saddle made by Adam Brothers—more than a mile over stones and brush and then into the alkali mud of White Bear.

I was so upset that I do not remember how we got back to camp. I found, when examining the saddle, that the leather

*Old Baldy, with Stan's younger brother, Billy, in the saddle, and sisters, Beryl and Darlene, standing guard.*
Author Photo

from the knob on the horn had been torn off. The lacing on the front left side of the rigging was broken. The leather on the pummel was scarred and so badly damaged that it would have to be replaced. Thank goodness, the leather roll around the top of the cantle was all right. Even the sheepskin padding looked as though it was ruined. I thought I might have to throw the entire thing away. But when the saddle dried and was cleaned with soap, it looked as though it could be repaired. The sheepskin padding, when brushed, was soft and fleecy.

That very day a big cow died out on the flats. After skinning out her back, the hide was fleshed and the hair removed. Then the hide was soaked in a rocksalt-saltpetre solution, and in a week, was cured and ready to be used in repairing the saddle.

With lace leather, cut from the hide, and a heavy strap of leather, we repaired the rigging. A single piece of the pliable rawhide was stretched over the pummel and pulled taut with rawhide thongs. Here and there, a few stitches were taken with a harness awl and heavy waxed thread to tidy up the loose ends.

After the saddle was reassembled, and all of the overlapping leather pieces had been put in place, it was left in the sun for the rawhide to harden and shrink. Then the pummel was scraped smooth with a piece of broken glass. The saddle looked better than ever. In my eyes, no one ever owned such a beautiful piece of riding equipment. Even now, after so many years, I remember the day that I bought it. It was the same day I had purchased my batwing chaps with silver conchas, and Jess, the big gentle saddle mare.

# Part Two
# Learning the Ropes

# The Night Hawk

The headquarters cook had the usual breakfast of steak, potatoes, and eggs ready, and he yelled to his helper, the bull cook, "Chuck's ready. Come and get it." The bull cook in turn rang the triangle outside, which brought all of the ranch-hands tumbling out of the bunkhouse or wherever else they might have been.

There were several large wash basins, pails of cold water, and soap and towels outside the kitchen door, and we all lined up for our turn to clean up before going into the dining room, presided over by Mr. Lair at the head of the table. Breakfast was hearty but did not last long, for there was much work to be done.

Already, near the blacksmith shop, the bed and chuck wagons had been dismantled. These extra heavy-duty wagons with four-inch iron tires were being completely rebuilt. The wooden wheels had dried some and shrunk, and this caused the tires to be loose and the spokes and felloes to have too much give. To correct this, the circumference of the tires had to be made smaller.

To accomplish this, a large wood fire was built on the ground. The tires were placed on this and heated as hot as possible. Then each tire was picked up by four men with tongs and part of it was placed in a hot coal fire in the forge and heated until white hot.

The tire was now placed in a large crimping machine with huge jaws that bit into it. The space between the jaws was about six inches, and a big lever was pressed down to shrink the space in the tire to the right amount. As each part was shrunk, it was pounded with a large hammer so it would keep its shape in proportion to the rest of the tire.

Usually the tire was hot enough that it expanded and could be fitted onto the wheel, but if it was too loose it had to be heated again. On the other hand, if the tire was too hot it might burn the wooden

*American Matador crew eating dinner with chuck wagon, bed wagon, and remuda in the background. The photo was taken near the town of Matador, Texas.*
Courtesy Opal Bradford

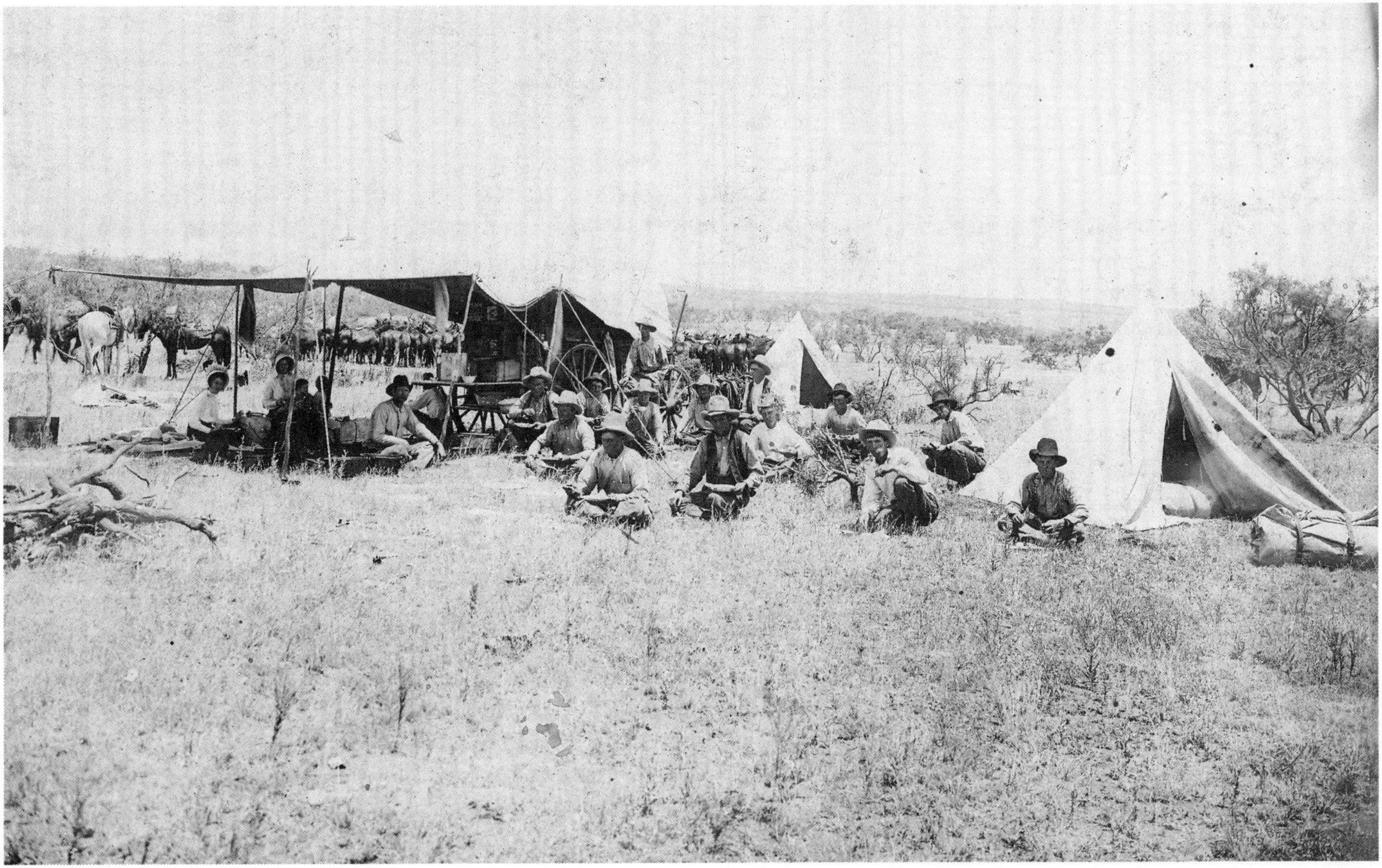

felloes, and so a good supply of water was kept handy to douse the hot spots.

The wagon boxes underwent a complete checkover as did the chuck-wagon cupboard, which had drawers facing out or back at the endgate end of a three-deck wagon box. The metal hoops that supported the canvas cover of the chuck wagon were also checked to ensure they were secure. Absolutely everything was gone over thoroughly so that nothing would break down for the next six months, especially during a long cattle trail drive.

There were so many items that needed attention: wooden water barrels, the outside brackets and fasteners that held them in place when travelling over rough prairie; also neck yokes, wagon poles, eveners, and whiffletrees; and the wheels needed greasing. The stove wagon, which went onto the reach by a clevis and chain behind the rear wheels of the chuck wagon, also was given attention. Harnesses and collars were repaired and oiled—nothing was missed.

The whole remuda of saddle and work horses was assembled, including the cripples and condemned bunch, in the home pasture so they were handy and needed no night hawk to herd them. Cy Thornton informed me that I would do the night-herding of the remuda when we got into the big summer pasture where we would go immediately after we left headquarters.

When moving camp, I helped harness and hitch up the bed-wagon horses and drove the wagon to the next camp site. When we arrived at the new camp on the trail, I got my bedroll out at once and put it under the bed wagon to keep it out of the sun or for cover in case it rained. Someone else took care of the bed-wagon horses so that I—the night hawk—could get as much sleep as possible. Later that day, when the tent was set up at the back of the chuck wagon, I moved into the far end, out of the way. It was always noisy, so it seemed I was constantly tired.

I night-hawked the better part of two summers at the Matador. During that time I discovered what solitude really meant. I learned about the stars and the moon—I had no watch but I always knew what time it was. I also grew to know instinctively where I was and where the camp was, even in total darkness. The remuda had to be "loose-herded" so the horses could graze unhampered. It was my responsibility to never lose a horse, so I continually had to check to see that none were missing. You could never count 125 horses in the dark, but there was a system that worked well. Horses are social, like most animals, and a remuda of

*Horses are social animals. Cy Thornton's horse was a patient animal, too.* Courtesy Opal Bradford

125 horses was made up of ten or fifteen cliques with five or ten horses in each. You got to know the cliques. This one probably had one white horse in it. Another clique had two white horses. Another one contained a bunch of bays, which were hard to see in the dark, so you put a bell on one of them.

Every horse herd had a few spoiled ones, such as a little sorrel that Mr. Lair called Baby Pony. The rest of us called him Blondie. Another spoiled brat was Painto. These two would leave the horse herd to go back to the wagon camp—maybe by now a mile or two away. A couple of bags of oats were kept in the bed wagon for reserve feed for some horse whose rider might have to go back to headquarters—fifteen or twenty miles away—on an emergency trip. Blondie and Painto knew where the oats were kept and would sneak back to camp to steal some. These rascals and some of their friends never went missing; we always knew where they were.

I had a favourite night horse—Old Star—all bay with a small white star on his forehead. He was sure-footed in the dark and a truly good friend. There was only one fault with his friendship. Each spring, after being free all winter, he would always try darn hard to buck me off when I rode him for the first time. He was a "switcher," too, even when there were no mosquitoes, and, typical of all switchers, he often danced on his hind legs when walking.

Often, on cold nights when there was little wind, I got off Old Star and lay on the ground. I would tie my reins together, slip them over my arms, and put my hands up my sleeves. Then I would lie all curled up, and on some occasions drop off to sleep for a moment or two. All the while Old Star would be grazing around me, often next to my face, his nose occasionally touching me. I could hear the curb bit in his mouth making metallic sounds. He was all over me and around me as I lay almost asleep, but never once did he step on me.

When it grew wintry cold, as it often did in late fall while rounding up a beef herd, I would ride into camp during the night a couple of times and curl up around the cookstove to get warm. On these occasions, I would eat the midnight lunch that the cook always made and have some coffee, which stayed warm on the back of the coal-fired stove.

I have many memories of those months of nighthawking: the cold, fatigue, sitting with a broken back on a grazing horse while a coyote howled from a nearby hill. Only a cowhand who has spent long hours in the big silence of the open range can understand.

# Flying Tails and Kicking Heels

Cy Thornton was in the large dip-vat corral, checking the horses. He roped these one by one and gave each a thorough examination. Those that checked out okay were put in one pen and the rejects in another. Some that had run for a year or more with the condemned had fully recovered from an injury or blemish and so were declared fit to be ridden.

There were many stories told and retold in the bunkhouse about some of these condemned, or crippled, horses. Several of them simply could not be broken into serviceable saddle horses or even to harness. I can think of three such unbreakable horses. They ran together at all times and when you rode toward them, even at a distance of a mile, they would gather on the top of a high hill and watch suspiciously as you approached. One could tell that they were snorting with nervousness. As if on a given signal, they would disappear almost instantly over the horizon, leaving only a memory of flying tails and manes.

I heard many bunkhouse yarns about a little brown Colorado pony called Bootjack that threw a tough bronco skinner, Byklum, into Bootjack Tank. In the process of doing this, Bootjack acquired his name, as well as a bad injury that placed him with the cripples for a couple of years.

Most of us were sitting on the top rail of the corral that nice evening and were quietly watching Cy go over the horses. Suddenly the rider next to me said, "Cy's got Bootjack." I noticed that the instant the foreman's loop fell over this little brown pony's head he knew he was captured, and obediently and meekly followed the rope right up to Cy.

The foreman ran his hands over Bootjack's legs and body, then looked up and said, "Stan, bring your bridle." Up until that moment it had never occurred to me that Cy would put this little rascal in my remount string. Anyway, whatever the boss said in those years, you said, "Yes, sir!"

So I had Bootjack. He was not at all "goosy" but real quiet and friendly. His head was so small I had to shorten the head stall on the bridle.

By the time I had Bootjack bridled and saddled, my rubbery legs had stiffened and my heart had again commenced to beat. However, when Cy said to me, very quiet and friendly-like, "Better ride him in the corral, Stan," I again started to quake. Pride finally forced me to rack the saddle back and forth by the horn to let Bootjack feel what my leather was like on his back.

Then I put my foot in the stirrup and swung on. At first he sort of felt the bit and I held his head up, then without spurring, we inched a foot or so ahead and then into a walk and trot. I breathed a sigh of relief—for now.

We returned that evening just at dark and turned the remuda loose in the small home pasture. I kept a night horse in the barn to round up the horses in the morning.

Breakfast at the Matador, no matter how long the day, was always completed just before sun-up. It rained all that night and was sprinkling hard in the morning, and the mud and manure in the corral had turned into about six inches of thick soup. The wet day also meant we would have to ride in our rain slickers.

In those years, raincoats were called "oil skins." They looked and felt like plastic, and rustled just as it does. This scared the dickens out of horses and encouraged them to buck, especially when it was the first time they had been ridden in the spring.

All the riders had caught, saddled, and mounted their horses just outside the corral gate, except Mr. Lair and me. Since Mr. Lair was so heavy, his saddle horses were in the 1,300-pound class. The "Old Man" caught and saddled his favourite horse, Snooks. No sooner was he in the saddle than Snooks looked around to make sure that there were a suitable number of spectators, then gave two or three good bucks and threw Legs right at my feet in the manure. Mr. Lair picked himself up out of the dripping manure and, still holding his riding reins, looked the horse eye to eye and said, "You danged old fool, Snooks. I've got a good notion to cave your ribs in."

Then it was time for the inevitable. There was no one left but me and Bootjack. I caught and saddled him, giving the cinch an extra tug or two on the latigo.

I opened the large iron gate and closed it carefully, letting Bootjack out.

A jury of my peers was waiting on horseback to judge what was about to happen. I looked for sympathetic eyes—there were none. I knew that honour demanded I ride clean and never, never pull leather.

I "cheeked" Bootjack, and in doing so, pulled his head my way as far as possible. I stepped in the stirrup, mounted, and screwed myself down in the saddle. Bootjack hesitated a moment, as much as to say, "Are you ready?" and then he shoved his head down between his front legs and simply exploded. He fishtailed and swapped ends, both at the same time. My east end went west and once, looking down, I could see the top of the barn beneath me—or so it seemed.

The river hills and breaks went round and round, and at this point Bootjack performed his specialty—the juggling act. This day he was particularly good, they say. His specialty consisted of repeatedly throwing me up and then catching me before I hit the ground. As spontaneously as he had exploded, he returned to the gentle, little brown pony who was one of the best cutting horses in our outfit.

We rode east on the river flat for a mile or two and then went up on top by one of the hay trails. Mr. Lair

*Lineup of cowboys, with one of the Matador chuck-wagon outfits in the background. The mules on the right pulled the chuck wagon and bed wagon.* Courtesy Opal Bradford

and Cy rode at the lead. It looked as though they were planning the work that had to be done. Today, we were going to go down into Nine- and Eleven-mile coulees to see if there were any stray cattle that might have been missed earlier. Mr. Lair said there were rumours that some had been seen.

As we came to Nine-mile, a few of the riders circled north around the head of it to go to Eleven-mile, farther on, and the rest of us dropped off the southerly edge at the west side. These large coulees were almost like mountain canyons. The place where we dropped over the rim was a straight descent of a couple of feet; then it became a slope of insecure rubble running at a very steep angle for what seemed to be a great distance.

It did not seem possible for a horse and rider to descend here. However, Jim Reynolds, the top hand, said this was about the only place to go down and that it was okay, if you just gave your horse his head. We worked these coulees thoroughly and until Mr. Lair was satisfied this part of the range was clear of cattle. It was late in the day when we arrived back at headquarters, where the cooks had an enormous meal ready for us.

By now we had heard the news that the Canadian government had given official notice they would not renew the lease on the six-township range that the Matador held and which terminated at the end of the current year, 1921.

We knew that as soon as everything was ready at headquarters, we would go north and cut out the beef so that the stockers could be trail-driven to the Matador ranch in the Belknap Reservation at Harlem, Montana.

We heard that a movie outfit run by a movie and rodeo promoter had been given the rights to film the drive. In exchange, his contract stipulated that he take over the expense and handling of the trail drive.

Ray Knight, from High River, Alberta, was well and favourably known for his successes in managing projects of this kind. The arrangement was that Mr. Knight would employ the Matador chuck-wagon outfit, including bed wagon and the remuda, saddle, and work horses. About seven or eight of the Matador ranch-hands were to go, including Cy Thornton, Jim Reynolds, Earl (I never did know his last name), Archie Hawes, who rode the rough string, myself, Jim Hayes, the cook, and maybe two or three others from the Matador crew.

The Knight outfit had their own chuck and bed wagons and remuda. Jim Hayes cooked for the two outfits once they were thrown together. He was assisted by the Knight cook. Barton, who was Knight's foreman, was to boss the whole show, and Jim Reynolds was to be the scout, or advance man, to locate water, grazing, and a place for the next night's camp, every twelve or fifteen miles along the trail.

Cy said I was to wrangle the remuda. On a trail drive this was an easy job, as after a few days on the trail the horses just followed the wagons on their own without being herded. The horse wrangler, the scout, the night hawk, and the last two riders in camp had to break up the old camp and set up a new one at the end of a day's travel. Jim Reynolds would lead. The cook, who drove four horses on the chuck wagon, came next. He was followed by the bed wagon, which was always driven by the night hawk, usually along a winding route to the next night's camp.

Cattle ranching is raising beef, which is sold by the pound. If a trail drive is not properly managed and the cattle are not handled right, thousands of pounds—and dollars—can be lost. Among cattlemen there were some who had the know-how or gift to boss a drive even over vast distances such as on the old Chisholm Trail from southern Texas to the northern markets, and the cattle even gained weight on the trail. Barton was such a trail boss.

# Preparing For the Trail

In August of 1920, the chuck wagon and crew had been repairing the dam at Bootjack Tank in the summer pasture. Joe and Lightfoot, my bed-wagon team of half-broken horses, had been used on a walking plough to break sod and on a slip scraper to haul dirt for fill.

They were driven by a quick-tempered and excitable cowhand named James Henson, whom we called "Swede." He should have driven the team gently but instead jerked them around until they were out of control and ran away with the scraper. There were a couple of riders nearby but it was too dangerous to get near the runaways as the scraper was flying around behind the terrified horses.

Finally the scraper blade stuck in the ground and the eveners broke, freeing the runaway team. It was easy to catch Joe and Lightfoot then. Cy Thornton and Mr. Lair had fired Swede right then and there; Swede's grudge against these men would follow him into the grave. But the damage had been done. The runaway had spoiled these half-broken horses.

In the spring of 1921, when things were being readied for the arrival of the Ray Knight outfit from High River, Joe and Lightfoot were put in a stall at the Matador headquarter barn. Physically, the team was evenly matched. Both were red roans with white faces and legs, sorrel manes and tails, and both had pink hooves, noses, and glass eyes.

The foreman asked Jim Reynolds to help me get Joe and Lightfoot into the barn as neither had been in one before. Joe, who was more docile, was roped first and did not put up much of a fight. Lightfoot, on the other hand, was almost impossible to handle. Jim snubbed him close to his big roping horse, Whiteman, and then, by force, dragged the frightened animal into the barn. By the time Lightfoot was tied securely in his stall beside Joe, he was dripping with sweat.

My job now was to handle these frightened horses as gently as possible for a couple of days. First I curried and brushed Joe from the next stall. Then, moving in beside him, it was not long before I could use the brush on his head and foretop. I could even get in front of Joe next to the manger and brush his right shoulder and neck. Harnessing and putting the collar and hames on was no problem. It was a relief to find that he was so gentle.

Next, I approached Lightfoot from under Joe's neck, slowly and carefully. He was terrified, and pulled mightily on the halter shank around his neck and through the ring on his rawhide halter, shaking his head violently. The manger to which he was tied groaned but was much too strong to break. All during this time he struck out at me with his forefeet and intermittently kicked with his hind. Fortunately the manger was at my back, and I tumbled into it before being injured.

We left the horses to quiet down but soon brought them hay and water in a bucket. Joe had a good drink and Lightfoot took a swallow or two and soon became quiet enough to harness. The horses were left in the barn all that day and night, and again the next day and night. We continued to bring them feed and water, and it was surprising how quickly this gentled them.

Meantime, Jim Hayes was loading his chuck wagon with food from the well-stocked commissary. Staples such as flour, sugar, salt, lard, butter, beans, and molasses were loaded first. Then the old rancher/pioneer dried fruits such as apples and apricots. Raisins and prunes were also included in large quantities. There was a large round of cheddar cheese and some canned goods including cases of jam, corn syrup, fruit, and beans for use in emergencies at a cold camp. Potatoes, carrots, turnips, and onions came from the root cellar, and several slabs of fat sow belly were added as well as some canned milk.

Cowhands have big appetites. Jim Hayes knew this and provided accordingly. The Matadors, wherever they were throughout the world, had an enviable record of having the best cooks and supplying them with plenty of good food to prepare. We were fortunate also in that Mr. Lair was an excellent cook and saw to it that we were well fed.

Jim Hayes was one of the best sourdough cooks around. He had two five-gallon earthen crocks and into these he put his sourdough starter—some dough from his last batch. To this he added just the right amounts of flour, sugar, and water. The mixture was left in the proper place for several hours in not too warm nor too cool a temperature, and from this came the most delicious flapjacks, hot buns, and the best bread you could ever imagine.

There were ongoing preparations for the bed wagon as well. Coal, wood, kerosene, and a few bags of oats were loaded. Because it was spring, and watering tanks or dams and springs were being repaired, we carried a walking plough and a slip scraper as well as some fire-fighting equipment such as gunny sacks and water pails to wet the sacks when flogging a prairie fire. As well, we carried a chain-link blanket that had an asbestos cover. This heavy, six-by-six-foot blanket was dragged over a fire line by two saddle horses. Behind them came men with wet gunny sacks to flog out the hot spots.

News reached us that the Ray Knight outfit would be arriving at Gas Springs in a day or two. Their foreman, Barton, had travelled faster than expected from his base at High River. Getting ready for the trail a day or two earlier than planned was no problem.

There were no cattle to herd and so there was plenty of help to hook up the horses on the wagons. Five or six hands harnessed and hooked up the four for the chuck wagon, driven by the cook. The leaders were Johnnie and Button, a light pair of harness horses who had been chuck-wagon leaders for years. On the nigh-pole side was the veteran, Old Shannon—a big sorrel of about 1,800 pounds. On the off-pole side, or left, was any big bronc that did not make it as a saddle horse. The halter shank on this usually unbroken horse was tied to the harness on Shannon, who, in turn, controlled his teammate. A few men helped hook up Joe and Lightfoot on the bed wagon, and held them for me until the whole outfit was ready to go.

Jim Hayes was an outstanding wagon driver. He always made sure his hat was secure, and when he got on the spring seat on the wagon he put his right foot down hard on the brakes. This was to put as much drag as possible on the load and slow it down from its beginning, hell-bent-for-leather pace. There was usually an outrider on each side of the wagon, and in the lead was either the foreman or our top hand, Jim Reynolds.

In the moments before we started on our wild and noisy race, the excitement stirred the blood of even the oldest cowhands. The wagon leaders, Johnnie and Button, and even Old Shannon, would tremble with anticipation like young thoroughbreds in the starting gate. I have never felt anything so rough as those wagons were in the first quarter of a mile, flying over the unbroken prairie.

This organized confusion is merely one of the reasons why the life of a cowpoke is preferable to that of a successful executive sitting behind a desk surveying his empire.

# Sourdough

2 large mealy potatoes, peeled and cut in half
2 tablespoons sugar
1 package dry yeast, dissolved in ¼ cup warm water
3 cups all-purpose flour, scoop measured
1 cup warm water

Place potatoes in a large saucepan with enough water to cover. Boil gently until the potatoes fall apart. Do not drain. Force through a sieve, liquid and all, and allow to cool to room temperature. Add water to the potatoes if necessary to make 3 cups. Pour into a large glass or ceramic bowl. Using a nonmetal spoon, stir in the sugar, dissolved yeast, and 2 cups flour. Beat until smooth and creamy. Cover with a clean kitchen towel and set in a moderately warm spot (about 70°Fahrenheit). Allow to stand for 24 hours, at which point the batter should smell pleasantly sour. Stir in the remaining cup of flour and 1 cup warm water. Cover with a towel and allow to stand at room temperature for 2 to 3 days. The longer it stands, the more assertive the flavour. Transfer the starter to a tightly covered glass or plastic container and store in the refrigerator. To use the starter, stir in any liquid sitting on the surface, measure out what you need, and allow it to come to room temperature. Replenish what you remove by stirring in equal parts of flour and water. (For example, if you remove 1 cup of batter, stir in ½ cup flour and ½ cup water.)

Reprinted from *Old Farmer's Almanac*, 1988. By Judy Gorman.

# Sourdough Pancakes

1½ cups all-purpose flour, scoop measured
1 tablespoon sugar
2 teaspoons baking powder
½ teaspoon baking soda
¾ teaspoon salt
1½ cups milk
2 large eggs
3 tablespoons butter, melted
1 cup sourdough, at room temperature

Combine flour, sugar, baking powder, soda, and salt in a large mixing bowl. Whisk to blend. In a separate bowl, whisk together the milk, eggs, and butter. Make a well in the dry ingredients and pour in the sourdough. Then add the egg mixture and stir with a wooden spoon until well moistened. The batter will contain some lumps. Place a griddle over medium-high heat. Brush the surface with vegetable oil or rub with a strip of uncooked bacon as the griddle warms. When the griddle is hot, stir the batter and add more milk if necessary to create a consistency like heavy cream. Ladle scant ¼ cupfuls onto the hot griddle. Cook until the bubbles around the outside edge are broken. Turn pancakes and cook the other side. Repeat with remaining batter, adding additional milk if needed to maintain proper consistency. Keep cooked pancakes warm until all are ready. Makes 12 large pancakes.

Reprinted from *Old Farmer's Almanac*, 1988. By Judy Gorman.

# First Impressions

It was hot, very hot! On the western horizon, heat waves were shimmering and dancing. Above this the mirrorlike sky seemed to reflect the scene below.

When our chuck-wagon outfit arrived at Gas Springs this day in the middle of May 1921, we set up camp some distance from the small pond near the springs so as not to keep the half-wild cattle away from water. The rope corral was stretched, and fresh saddle horses were staked out on tethers. The sides of the tent were rolled up four or five feet.

After our noon meal, we were lying back against our bedrolls in the shade with the light breeze blowing through the tent. Though warm, we were quite comfortable. There we dozed and dreamily gazed westward for signs of the arrival of Ray Knight's outfit from High River.

A horse and rider appeared in the mirage, large and ghostlike. They were coming directly toward us, yet did not seem to be making any progress in our direction. I imagined what the horse would look like as he laboured in the heat: nostrils flaring and blowing his nose as he tossed his head and took in great gulps of air.

Probably, it was when the horse and rider crossed over the true horizon that they disappeared. It was an hour later before they could be seen as small figures in the distant west. As they moved through the sparsely scattered herds, the grazing cattle parted, allowing the pair a straight run east.

We could tell when the rider first spotted our camp. Before this, his course would have brought him too far south. His shift to the north was taken abruptly about a mile and a half west, and then he brought his horse to a walk. By the time he rode into Gas Springs,

The Matador remuda in a rope corral on the Saskatchewan River flats, six miles east of the Saskatchewan Landing river crossing. Stan is on the far left riding Few Brains, a horse who enjoyed jumping sideways when his rider dismounted. Cy Thornton can be seen walking toward Stan. The blazed white face of Old Baldy is visible to Cy's right. Next to Baldy are Johnnie and Button, the lead team for the chuck wagon. The horse with his head over the back of Button is Painto. Old Buck, one of Stan's night horses, is standing broadside, out in the open. Jim Reynolds is roping in the corral. The large man in the centre is Ray Knight and beside him is Barton, Knight's foreman. Pete Laplante stands to the right. Man on far right is unknown. Author Photo

his horse had started to dry and cool down.

Our visitor dismounted a little stiffly, put out his hand to our foreman, and said, "They call me Barton. I'm the foreman of the Ray Knight Horse Ranch."

His next remark was, "I could sure use a good swig on one of those canvas water bottles hanging under the wagon."

Wiping the sweat from his face and forehead with a large red handkerchief, a look of relief and satisfaction passed over him as the cool water wet his parched throat.

Barton said he had hoped to have the Ray Knight outfit into Gas Springs earlier that day but they had met with an unexpected delay. As he was having a large piece of Jim Hayes's dried apple pie, cheese, and coffee, Barton kept looking west, but it was about two hours before his outfit appeared in the distance. Cy Thornton immediately rode out to guide them to our camp.

Supper that night gave Hayes an opportunity to show off his skills. He was a good cook and knew it. He called on several of the Matador men to help lay out the huge spread he had whipped up to show how talented he really was. In appreciation, we all helped him wash the dishes.

Evidently Barton asked Cy Thornton to have someone ride down that evening to the Matador headquarters on the river, about fifteen or eighteen miles southwest, to let Mr. Lair know that the Knight outfit had arrived. He was also to let the camera and movie people know that the Great Roundup at Gas Springs would commence in the morning so that company officials could be present at this important event.

Our Archie Hawes was delegated to make the ride. Archie rode our rough string and could really sit a tough bronc. He selected a sturdy little bay that he had partly broken the year before. It was the first time this spring the horse would be ridden. I caught and saddled my favourite night horse, Old Star, to haze for Archie as his bronc was cut loose.

We should have snubbed the bronc to my saddle on Old Star and had Archie mount him from there. But Jim Reynolds and Archie roped the bronc in the corral and after a struggle got the little horse out in the open. There, Jim put a gunny-sack blindfold over the horse's head. He had a firm grip on the bronc's nose and had twisted an ear round and round, then bit the ear with his teeth and held on.

The horse stood still as Archie saddled and bridled him, then climbed aboard. Jim cut the little bay loose and what happened next can hardly be described.

First the little hay-burner reared straight up on his hind legs, waving his forefeet. It appeared he would fall on his back, fatally injuring Archie. Fortunately, the horse kept his balance, falling forward. With his head down and mouth open, the frightened pony let out piteous roars. He was crazed with terror and his bucking was so violent that no one could have ridden him.

Archie's stay on the hurricane deck was quite heroic. Sitting nearby on Old Star, I got a good view of the setting sun beneath Archie as he sailed skyward.

At that very moment, Old Star caught me by surprise when he decided that he, too, would not submit without a fight. This gentle old friend forgot about the times he looked out for me when we were nighthawking the remuda on a stormy night.

His first pitch was so unexpected that it loosened me in the saddle and my hat flew off. However, Star was not a hard horse to ride, even when he bucked his best. He looked tougher to ride than he really was.

I finally pulled the old fellow's head up and he quit bucking. Looking back, I could see our two crews lying back against their bedrolls, enjoying the show that Archie, Jim, and I had put on. What I did next I have tried ever since to explain in my own mind. My hat was lying nearby on the grass. I rode Star next to the hat, which was on the downhill side, and holding the horn on the saddle, reached down to retrieve it. Of course, it was much too far and I nearly fell off the horse. I had a hard time pulling myself back in the saddle.

At the time (and now), it all looked so silly. I was not accustomed to being on centre stage and was probably embarrassed, or maybe I was just trying to say, "Oh, shucks, you should see me ride a tough one." Later, even when I knew our crew had not felt we had disgraced them, I still had an uneasy feeling about it.

Archie, meanwhile, was hobbling in from where he had been thrown. He was a sorry sight indeed, limping along in his high-heeled riding boots. I rode out and rounded up his riderless bronc, who came back to the remuda without any problems.

This time the bronc was snubbed to my saddle and Archie mounted from there. The little bay jerked around but could not buck with his head so closely and solidly tied. We took Archie a couple of miles toward headquarters before turning him loose, and he arrived back in Gas Springs at one or two o'clock the next morning on a very tired but well-broke pony.

# The Great Roundup

The southern range of the Coteau Hills lay to the north of Gas Springs. The elevation of the highest hills was probably 3,000 feet. From the top of one of those pinnacles, to the south, you could see the great gorge of the Saskatchewan in the distance, with its canyonlike coulees.

The stony hills of Bone Pile Ridge were twenty miles west, running north and south, and between the Coteau Hills and this ridge was the lower Sanctuary Valley. To the east, the hills were lower, and cattle could be seen grazing for miles in all directions.

Gas Springs was an unusual watering place for the several thousand head of cattle in the north Matador pasture. The spring was south of centre in an almost flat saucerlike depression about three miles in diameter. Good, clear water came up from the middle of a small but very deep pond. The level of the pond, during the time I rode for the Matador, never seemed to vary in depth. Probably the gravel base at the perimeter of the pond controlled the water level by draining off the excess. This gravel base, hard and firm, kept the pond from being trampled into a mud puddle by the stock that came to drink.

On a clear, windless evening when not a ripple disturbed the pond, one could see the great volume of water rising from the depths to the surface. About once every minute, as the incoming water broke the surface of the glassy pool, there came with it a big bubble or belch of natural gas.

There was no algae in the pond, and gas coming into it must have been siphoned off from some pool in the lower bowels of the earth. The rising gas likely had an aerating effect that kept the water clear and clean.

It was nine miles west and an equal distance east to the boundaries of the pasture surrounding Gas

*Cutting out beef at the Gas Springs roundup. Note the riders among the cattle. Beef steers that are cut from the main herd are being guided toward the smaller herd at the upper right. This smaller herd of beef is called the "cut." The rider on the left is Stan Graber on Old Buck.* Author Photo

Springs. To the north, it was five miles and south one mile. Aside from this central location, and a flat plain on which to work a large herd of cattle, this was the perfect place for the Great Roundup.

The deep prairie wool of buffalo, blue-stem, and grama grass, along with plenty of good water, provided a pasture where cattle could be held and worked for days without loss of weight.

Cy Thornton had already explained to his crew that the Matador riders would sweep the entire pasture of cattle in one day. This would mean a very long sit in the saddle and the working of two or three fresh horses each before the stock had all been gathered at Gas Springs. Barton and his Ray Knight men did not know the country nor the isolated parts of the range where some of the cattle were likely to be, so his outfit remained at Gas Springs, herding the remuda, and ready to circle the roundup of cattle as soon as they had been gathered.

By 4 A.M. Jim Reynolds and five other cowhands, including myself, were riding west in the dark. Just before daybreak, we reached the west fence. Three of us rode north and three south, along the fenceline. We dropped off about a mile apart before starting east. On most summer days, cattle drive easier against the wind than down wind, especially if there are flies or mosquitoes. This day, there was a light northwest breeze. At the beginning, the cattle moved slower from the west going east than when driven in the opposite direction. It seems odd, but often, when large herds of cattle begin moving in one direction, other herds start to line up, one by one, and move along with them. Sometimes, when I looked down from higher ground, I could see cattle all moving in the same direction in a very orderly manner—and this without a rider on horseback in sight. Most likely such herds were going to water, but occasionally, they moved in this fashion without any apparent reason.

Once they got started, the cattle moved east quite willingly, and by seven o'clock there were dozens of strings of white-faced, Matador Herefords on a six-mile front, all heading toward the rising sun. Such a glorious sight we shall never see again.

This morning I was riding Blackbird, the best all-around saddle horse I have ever ridden. He was tall—about seventeen hands—and good looking. He wore a jet black shiny coat with a short tail, mane, and foretop, and was fairly heavy boned, with small hooves and lightly feathered fetlocks. He was deep chested, short bodied, and built for endurance. The most amazing thing about this great saddle horse was that he was a natural-born pacer, a "single footer." He was very easy to ride on long circles with his graceful, waltzing pace. Blackbird was gentle but spirited, and his quickness in working cattle often made it difficult to keep a secure seat in the saddle. He never seemed to tire, and, with it all, was stylish and classy.

Gradually, after a long day and much hard riding, the cowhands of the Matador pushed together three thousand, four thousand, and eventually a total of six thousand head of Herefords. The cattle had been reluctant to leave their home pasture in their range around Basin Springs. We had the same problem at Laidly Springs to the northwest. As the herds were funnelled into the holding grounds at Gas Springs, they were circled closely and gathered into the Great Roundup by Barton and his Ray Knight crew. By two o'clock that afternoon, the last white-faced steer had been pushed into a great milling herd.

None of the Matador men had eaten since three-thirty that morning. After ten hours of hard riding in the dust, we were dirty, hungry, thirsty, and dead tired.

As I looked up I saw Mr. Lair circling the cattle and riding toward me. He suggested that I get something to eat, have a short rest, get my cutting horse, Bootjack, and return to the roundup to work with him cutting cattle.

My weariness and hunger disappeared. I couldn't believe I would have a chance to work so closely with Mr. Lair. I didn't even notice when Bootjack bucked as usual; I felt only impatience with his fooling around.

There were fewer beef or mature steers ready for market in the roundup than stockers going to Montana, so our work today was to cut out those ready for sale.

As we rode through the cattle, Mr. Lair would show me a steer that was to be removed from the herd. I never took my eyes off the animal and would gently guide Bootjack until he, too, recognized the steer to be cut. Then this little brown pony, almost without guidance, started working the steer to the edge of the roundup, then out into the open. At this point, the steer made frantic dashes back and forth to get back into the herd, but his every move was intercepted by Bootjack. At times we raced up and down, stopping instantly at the end of each dash. Now and then the two animals stood face to face and stared at one another. Bootjack, almost sitting on his hind legs, with his forelegs spread in front, made ready to swing instantly right or left. This little master of his trade thoroughly

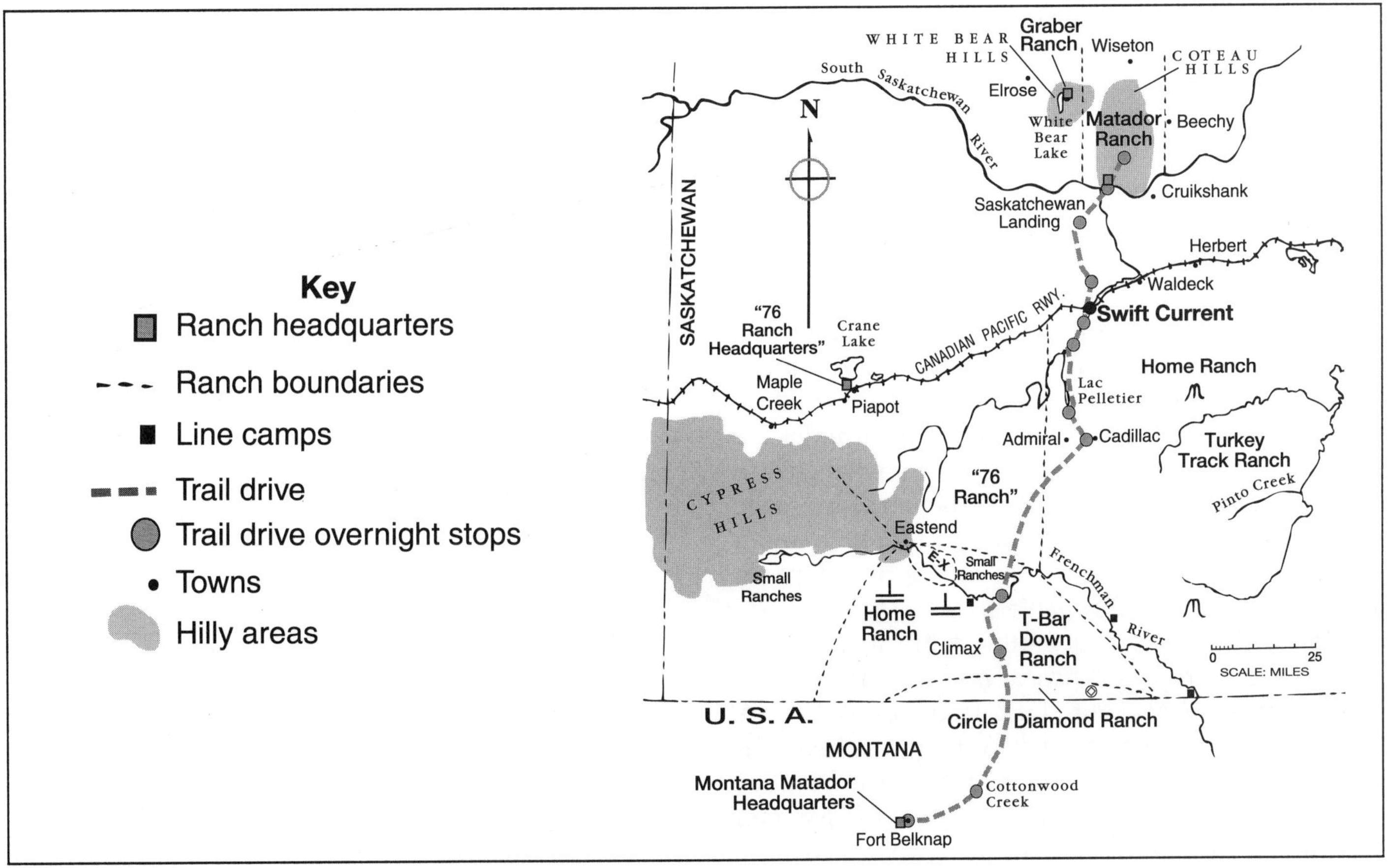
Key
Ranch headquarters
Ranch boundaries
Line camps
Trail drive
Trail drive overnight stops
Towns
Hilly areas
WHITE BEAR HILLS
Graber Ranch
Wiseton
COTEAU HILLS
South Saskatchewan River
Elrose
White Bear Lake
Matador Ranch
Beechy
N
Cruikshank
Saskatchewan Landing
Herbert
Waldeck
Swift Current
SASKATCHEWAN
"76 Ranch Headquarters"
Crane Lake
CANADIAN PACIFIC RWY.
Maple Creek
Piapot
Lac Pelletier
Home Ranch
Admiral
Cadillac
Turkey Track Ranch
Pinto Creek
CYPRESS HILLS
"76 Ranch"
Eastend
E-X
Small Ranches
Frenchman River
Small Ranches
Home Ranch
T-Bar Down Ranch
Climax
0
25
SCALE: MILES
U. S. A.
Circle Diamond Ranch
MONTANA
Montana Matador Headquarters
Cottonwood Creek
Fort Belknap

enjoyed the excitement and chase. His ears were alternately going forward and backward; his eyes were shining. Even though I had a firm grip on the saddle horn, his quickness made him hard to ride.

All during this time, Mr. Lair, in his high, penetrating southern drawl, was continuously scolding or praising me. This day I received a college education in judging beef and handling them with the least stress.

Jim Reynolds, Cy Thornton, and, of course, Mr. Lair and I were working beef out of the roundup. There was a steady string of big, fat steers going to the cut, about half a mile northeast. Eventually the time came when there were no prime animals left in the Great Roundup. The Herefords remaining were only those stockers to be trailed to Montana and a few cripples that could be cut out as the Montana animals were counted or tallied.

The procedures and methods of handling big herds of stock on large ranches was the same, whether it be in lower Texas, South Dakota, or Saskatchewan. To arrive at an accurate count or tally of a herd, the standard procedure was to drive the cattle between two or more cowhands. Today, Cy, Jim, and Mr. Lair were doing the counting. Each had his rope down and as the cattle went between them, they counted. At each one hundred, they tied a knot in the rope and signalled to one another. When the tally was completed, a comparison was made of each count to arrive at the total—a simple and accurate method of taking an inventory.

The cattle, most of this warm day, had been held without water or grazing. When the beef herd was no longer circled by riders, it quickly strung out toward Bootjack Dam to the northwest. After watering the stockers at Gas Springs, these steers were driven south about a mile to the nearest gate into the Matador south winter pasture. There they were turned loose to graze and bed down for the night.

The quiet of a prairie evening and a full moon rode with us as we jogged back to our bedrolls at the wagon, ready for a good night's sleep.

# Saying Goodbye to a Cowboy

Obituary written for J.R. Lair by rancher Pete Perrin, March 1940.

Many who knew the veteran cowman will sincerely regret to learn that John Roscoe (Legs) Lair of Swift Current, Saskatchewan, has been called by the grim reaper at the age of seventy-four.

Widely known, especially among those interested in the cow business from the Canadian Prairies as far south as the state of Texas, few knew him by other than "J.R," or the more common "Legs."

Legs was all man. The first time you met him you would probably eye him from the top of his hat to the soles of his boots, and you would surmise that, after all, the guy who nicknamed him didn't have to be too danged intelligent to find a suitable name.

Legs stood six feet, six inches tall in his socks and weighed well over two hundred pounds. As conspicuous as Legs's physical appearance was, it was not uncommon to hear him before seeing him. He was a big man with a big man's voice. After hearing his voice once you could not mistake him among a million.

Legs was a man with a mind of his own, and seldom did anyone change it. He was honest and well-liked by everyone. In common with many from the old school, he firmly believed that a man's word of honour was as good as his name on paper. His great hobby was hounds, and he was a genuine lover of that particular breed of dogs. Nothing could stir Legs like the prospect of a good run. For a man of his size, he was unusually easy on horse flesh, but speed and rough country were forgotten when following his dogs in a race. He would as soon run a coyote as eat.

Legs's first acquaintance with Canada was in 1912 when the Matador Land and Cattle Company sent him to manage their holdings on the north side of the South Saskatchewan River, about thirty miles north of Swift Current. He had been with the Matador practically since boyhood. He held this position until 1922, when owing to the treacherous Canadian winters and the increasing difficulties of bringing cattle across the border from the south, the Matador Company pulled out of Canada.

Legs cursed the cold Canadian winters after arriving here from Texas, and for a time it was hard to convince him that anyone but the Indians and Eskimos could manage to live here. But he stayed long enough to get range broke. Legs remained at the old Matador headquarters camp until 1925, when he bought a little ranch for himself near the main line of the CPR about fifteen miles west of Swift Current. There he raised a small bunch of Shorthorn cattle until his death.

Since the time he was employed by the Matador he "batched." One never rode away from Legs's door hungry. The latch string hung on the outside, and his coffee pot stood on the stove. And what coffee it was. As the saying goes, "It would float a spur rowel."

Even though Old Legs has gone to join the greatest roundup of all, many pleasant memories of him remain, and many times will his name be spoken around cow camps and the ranges he once called home.

*Legs (the Old Man) Lair riding his favourite horse, Snooks, and accompanied by his ever-present wolf hounds. Although he carried a lariat on his saddle, he never used it because he believed it frightened his pampered saddle horses.* Author Photo

# Part Three
# Dusty Trails

# Swimming the Saskatchewan

The song of a meadowlark drifted to us on a friendly breeze. It was sunrise and the cheery song forecast that the day would be clear and sunny. By 10 A.M. at Gas Springs, the professional photographers, with their still cameras, were jubilant. Their light meters had indicated conditions were ideal for taking pictures of the roundup. Several photographers had their moving picture cameras set up on tripods and were stationed on high points above the crooked, deep coulee our outfit took from the high country down to the river flats of the Saskatchewan.

In places, the hills were so steep that every wagon had to have one of its rear wheels rough-locked with a logging chain. The half-broken horses pulling the wagons sat back in their breeching to keep the wagons from running away. Even then, the horses slid at times when things got rolling too fast. Jim Hayes led the way with his four horses. He followed the dim hay trails, dodging rock outcroppings as he chose the best path on the way down.

Following the wagons was the horse herd. For many of the old mustangs in the remuda, home was near the chuck wagon. When the wagons moved out, they picked up their heads and obediently followed. There was great variety in their ancestry and colouring. Many were sorrels and chestnuts, some were tough blue buckskins, others smoky duns and bays, all with that black stripe down their backs. A few had zebralike markings on their legs. They say these buckskins are descendants of the Berber horses brought to Mexico from Spain and Morocco by Cortez. The horse herd also included red roans, fancy paints, shiny blacks and bays, and many silvery whites and dapple greys. Two good blue roan ponies in my string were named Creepy and Donor, both wearing Colorado brands.

Next in line, and leading the cattle drive, was Jim Reynolds, riding point. Two hundred yards behind Jim were the uncertain herd leaders. This first day it was too early for a steer to establish his dominance as a leader. They were timidly and suspiciously following Jim, their heads down, smelling the ground at each step. The two cowhands riding swing in the vanguard of the herd had to continuously break up the huddling leaders. Progress to the river was slow, but at the beginning of the drive that was to be expected.

Before the cattle arrived at the river, the two chuck wagons and the Knight bed wagon had already set up camp near the headquarters buildings in the small home pasture.

At the cattle crossing on the north side of the river, there was a steep cutbank running up from the water. The west end of the cutbank gradually sloped up to the flat above. It was here where the cattle went down. The bank grew steeper and narrower to the east. At the narrowest, easterly end of the cutbank, there was a steep opening where the steers could go to the top and escape swimming the river. We placed the Matador bed wagon at this spot as an anchor for the rope corral. We hoped that this, along with the remuda and the riders changing horses, would serve as a barrier and keep the cattle from escaping.

But it did not work that way. The milling cattle down at the water's edge kept crowding those above until their only way out was to rush by the wagon, rope corral, and the cowhands trying to hold them. For three days we tried unsuccessfully to get the steers to swim across the Saskatchewan. The two Laplante boys and their elderly father were there with boats, but even these experienced boatmen seemed unable to help.

To add to that problem, the river suddenly rose in flood, and there were whole families of visitors and spectators in buggies and wagons coming from miles around. There were Model T Fords, and farm dogs, and their owners on horseback, some among the cattle.

The situation was one of confusion and frustration. Matador men and horses were exhausted. There seemed to be no solution.

Isidore Laplante, Senior, had served as guide for Murdo Mackenzie in 1903 when Mackenzie decided to lease the Matador land from the Canadian government. From that time until 1913, cattle from lower Texas were shipped by the Matador to Waldeck, ten miles east of Swift Current. Finished beef was shipped out through Waldeck each fall in this same time period. Going and coming, the stock had to swim the Saskatchewan, and, always, Mr. Laplante was there with his boat to assist. In 1921 he was the only one there who had experience swimming cattle across this broad, swift waterway, and we needed him.

The steel went through on the Elrose line in 1912,

the same year J.R. Lair is said to have come to Canada from Texas to manage the Saskatchewan ranch. Wiseton was three stations east of Elrose on the CN railroad. It was two or three miles east of the station of Wiseton that the railroad built stockyards to hold 3,000 to 3,500 head of cattle to accommodate the shipping of Matador stock. Shipping from Wiseton rather than Waldeck meant that the stock no longer had to swim the river.

In those years, when railroads were being built across the prairies, it was customary for them to build small stockyards at shipping points about twenty-five miles apart, usually on the boxcar siding close to the station house. The Matador shipping business required a large space near water and grazing. The stockyards built for the Matador had a long loading platform at boxcar or cattlecar level, running the full length of the pens. There were two loading chutes and ramps to assist in quick loading and to handle the usual four or five trainloads of steers as they arrived or were dispatched over the period of a week.

In the larger pens, the cattle were worked on horseback, but in the smaller pens, nearer the loading chutes, we worked on foot with a long slim prod pole, hence "cowpokes" or "cowpunchers." If one of these wild range-raised Texas steers was by itself it would inevitably charge, and it required youth and active footwork to avoid being injured. One never tried to handle one or two animals if they were the only ones in the pen. You opened the gate and let them escape. Then the riders on horseback drove ten or fifteen other steers into the loading pens. In these numbers, they could be worked quite safely on foot.

While we were loading the trains, the townsfolk of Wiseton came to watch; families would sit for hours on the top rails of the yards. Cy Thornton had a twinkle in his eye for the ladies and often put on a special show with his prod pole for some pretty miss who happened to smile in his direction. He truly became a "matador" as he isolated some lone steer and nimbly stepped aside as it charged. Though Cy was quite stout and not exactly young, he managed to put on quite a performance.

It must have been shyness or reluctance to interfere that prevented Laplante from making any suggestions that spring in 1921 when the Matador and Ray Knight men struggled to get the cattle to swim the Saskatchewan. But after three days of watching the confusion, the eighty-year-old Metis finally spoke up. Mr. Laplante told our manager that 3,500 head of

*Trying to get 3,500 head of cagey cattle to swim the broad Saskatchewan was no easy task. Not until Isidore Laplante, an elderly Metis with years of experience swimming cattle, suggested that the men break the cattle into herds of two and three hundred were the Matador men able to convince the animals to cross.* Author Photo

cattle could not be forced to swim such a broad expanse of fast water in one herd. He suggested the cattle be divided into bunches of two hundred. The smaller numbers could easily be forced across the river.

In the very early hours of the fourth day at the river (about 22 May) Mr. Laplante's plan was put into effect. After that we had no problems convincing the cattle to swim the river in smaller groups.

Cy Thornton was so sure all the cattle would be on the south side of the river today that he had us break camp and take the wagons and remuda across on the ferry at the Saskatchewan Landing, six miles west, and then set up a new camp at a big slough in the high country above the river, directly south of the river crossing.

When we first pulled out of Gas Springs, a seventeen-year-old rider called Pistol joined us. He was the nephew of Barton, the Ray Knight foreman. Already Pistol was an experienced bronc rider, as he would have to be on the staff of the Ray Knight horse outfit. He was large and strong for a man of his age. Other riders in his outfit said he had been on many wild horse chases to capture stock for the professional stampedes and rodeos that were staged across western Canada by Ray Knight.

These wild mustangs came from the open ranges of western Alberta and the big empirelike interior valleys of British Columbia. They were wonderful creatures. Most were direct descendants of Appaloosa horses that had escaped from northern Idaho and eastern Washington state and went wild. Horse ranching, and especially running wild horses, required good saddle stock. A rider did not have a big string of remounts, probably three to a rider was about the right number. Each was ridden hard and grain fed. In fact, even the harness horses were grain fed on the Knight ranch because horse herds on the trail covered long miles. Grass-fed saddle horses carrying riders did not have the stamina or endurance to outrun a wild horse herd.

From now until we reached the Montana border, I was the horse wrangler and Pistol was the night hawk. We became good friends and I enjoyed working with this pleasant young man. This first night, as I turned the remuda over to Pistol, the horses were grazing over the healing wagon ruts of the Battleford Trail, once a military route from Swift Current to old Battleford. Pistol told me the next morning that during the black, sombre night, he had seen the ghosts of those who had travelled this old trail and had never returned.

# Along the Old Battleford Trail

The days were growing longer as we made our way south. The dry warm weather that May made night-herding almost pleasant.

I couldn't help but compare this drive to an earlier cattle drive in the latter part of November 1920, when we had taken 3,000 beef steers to our shipping pens at Wiseton. The cattle were being shipped live to Great Britain. The Wiseton stockyards were forty miles north of the east Basin Gate out of the Matador summer pasture from where the trail drive began.

*After a long first day on the trail, we camped at a small lake that cold November evening. The day was short and overcast. It was already dark when we set up camp by the light of coal-oil lanterns. Wooden pegs, used for the guy ropes on the tent and the rope corral, splintered as we tried to drive them into the frozen ground; it was heavy work with a sledge hammer to drive in the iron pegs we had to use instead. All hands on middle and last guard quickly hit the sack.*

*I was on the middle or second guard—10 P.M. to 2 A.M.—and it seemed I had just fallen asleep when I was awakened by one of the fellows on first guard. He said there was a blizzard raging and the cattle had not bedded down. They were gradually moving downwind, growing more and more out of control.*

*Old Buck, one of my night horses, was tethered nearby, already saddled. His bridle was in its place on the wagon where I could easily find it in the dark. The herd was downwind. It was pitch black. Riding into the darkness with the wind in my back, I finally heard the cattle bawling, and in a few minutes I caught up with the herd. Hazing in long strings, I eventually came upon the riders on the downwind side. You could smell the steam and heat rising from the milling cattle.*

*All the riders had their ropes down and were popping*

them, and we were all hollering. But the herd gradually and relentlessly worked downwind.

By about 8:30 A.M., the cattle had drifted and milled south and were trapped against our north fence. Before daybreak we let them thin out so when they came to the fence, it held them.

By splitting the riders into two groups and circling east and west we gathered all the cattle into one herd. We had not lost one of them.

Something I will always remember as we returned to the chuck wagon to eat and get fresh horses was the trampled trail we had made as we followed the milling cattle during the night. The area was much wider than would be expected, and where there had been grass and snow, there was now only a greenish tinge of short stubble and manure.

When I think about it, I realize how sure-footed those Colorado mustangs were. I never in many years on the range had a night horse fall, even when riding at breakneck speed in total darkness. If one had fallen, an injured rider in the path of a milling herd would have been trampled to a pulp.

*A typical Matador wagon, located in an isolated corner of the pasture. The photo was taken on the Matador in Texas.* Courtesy Opal Bradford

With the Matador and Ray Knight outfits, there was plenty of help for each of the three night guards. There were also extra riders to loose-herd the steers as soon as they got up from their beds to graze in early morning.

This early grazing period or "jingle" was a busy time for riders: they had to have breakfast, change horses, and ready things for a quick breakup of camp.

Most of the work breaking camp involved loading equipment into the wagons. This was done by our scout, the cook, the horse wrangler, and the last two riders in for breakfast. As soon as breakfast was finished, the fire in the cook's stove was put out and the stove was loaded into its cart. The cart went onto the reach of the chuck wagon by a clevis and chain. The cupboard doors at the rear of the wagon box were closed with clamps. Meanwhile, the harness horses for the wagons were caught and harnessed. As usual, Johnnie and Button, the cook's lead team, were anxious to get going, as was Old Shannon on the pole.

The bed-wagon team of Joe and Lightfoot was harnessed and hooked up. The last thing to do was to take down the rope corral. The ropes had to be coiled carefully and placed properly in the bed wagon. The posts and pegs of the rope corral were put with the ropes so there would be no confusion when the corral was set up at the next camp.

We knew the place for every item as we loaded the wagons, and if we were not sure, we quickly found where it should go. The tents and bedrolls were packed just so in the bed wagon. All this apparent confusion was really a precise system learned by generations of experiences on cattle drives.

Men held the horses until Jim Hayes got his hat on straight and the bed-wagon team got in place. We pulled out of there so fast it was almost as though Jim Reynolds had shot a starting pistol.

On our way out we passed over the Battleford Trail and moved west of it a quarter of a mile. We travelled parallel to the old trail on unbroken prairie to our next camp.

Our next watering and camping site was twelve miles south and east near a big spring on the west side of a small lake. There were large bulrushes on the east side of the lake, and when we rode our horses near the rushes we discovered it was very boggy there. It is amazing how half-wild, range-raised cattle are able to sense where they might get bogged down and avoid these places even when very thirsty.

But this evening one steer got stuck in the bog.

Fortunately, the saddle horses had some good footing nearby and were able to pull him out. Since the steer had only been bogged down a short time he was not tired, and gave his benefactors a hard time getting the ropes off him.

Pulling the big steer out of one of those blue sand bogs after he had mired himself down to the ears surely tested the rigging on even the best of saddles. Old Buck could drag a steer heavier than he was quite easily in a sort of sideways shuffle. He sure could make saddle leather squeak.

The Battleford Trail has an interesting history. The first recorded traveller on it from north to south was a man by the name of Marchand. He travelled south from old Fort Battleford to Swift Current in 1883. At Swift Current he had the first ferry built for use at the landing crossing. The ferry was nine feet by eighteen feet and was hauled from Swift Current to the river by thirty-five horses. There are stories of many folks inexperienced in pioneer prairie living going north from Swift Current, ill-equipped and suffering untold hardships in their quest for opportunity and free land. Some started on the road with an unborn child whose mother had to be assisted at birth by some passing Indian. Many got lost on the trail in a severe winter and froze to death. Then they were found far off the trail in a melting snowbank with the frozen tears of despair on their cheeks. (It is no wonder young Pistol had sensed the presence of these unfortunate souls so vividly the night before.)

The Battleford Trail had served as a military road during the Riel Rebellion. Colonel Otter and his cavalry travelled along it on their way to relieve Fort Battleford, which was under siege during the rebellion. His troops had camped for the night at a big spring, just off the trail.

This large spring burst out of a short ravine on the eastern ramparts of the Three Bar Hills, four miles west of the northern shores of White Bear Lake. In the evening a wandering band of Indians threatened to attack Otter's troops. The cavalry dug defensive trenches on the slopes close to the spring, but the Indians did not attack. Since then, the spring has been known as Otter Springs.

The Royal North-West Mounted Police patrolled the territories between Swift Current and Fort Battleford east and west from the Battleford Trail. Each officer had a circuit of homesteaders and ranchers to visit—especially during the cold winters—to make sure that all was well.

I remember our family sitting around the kitchen stove in our homestead home one wintry evening when I was a child. When a knock sounded on the door, my father quickly opened it wide. Standing there was a Mountie holding the reins of his horse. The young man wore a large buffalo-hide coat, hat, and gauntlets. The high collar on his coat was covered with hoarfrost from his breath. When invited in, he left the door slightly open, as he continued to hold the riding reins of his horse. Father put on his outdoor clothing and took the officer's horse to the barn to be fed and watered.

Mother assisted the young man in removing his outer clothing and even his calf-length boots and spurs. She had a large pair of moccasins to help warm his cold feet.

I remember sitting back, no doubt with wide eyes, watching Mother as she made our guest welcome. She went to our coldroom under the stairway to get some venison steaks for his supper. This handsome young fellow, whom I had never seen before, and have never seen since, made such a lasting impression on me that I have never forgotten him. He wore the mantle of authority vested in him by his Majesty King Edward VII (1901–1910) with wisdom, kindness, and courtesy.

The old Battleford Trail also told tales of success and happiness. Great dynasties were often built by the venturesome. Those who travelled over it left evidence in the prairie sod of their passing. On this cattle drive we also felt the spirit of those happy voyagers as we journeyed south toward the Big Sky Country of Charles Russell and Montana.

*Cy Thornton, about 1918.* Courtesy Opal Bradford

# The Vanishing Crew

The steers leading the trail drive made their way over the horizon on the high and long hill north of the city of Swift Current. By late afternoon the cattle were no longer a herd but rather a winding, snaking column, six wide, extending from its vanguard far back to its tail end, or "drag," a distance of two or three miles.

Already the chuck wagon and horse herd were camped near water west of Swift Current on good grazing land (considering how near it was to town).

Our scout, Jim Reynolds, had returned from the wagon camp to check that the trail drive was making good progress. He saw to it that there were riders opposite each other all along the long column of cattle.

The swing riders were in the vanguard. Along the sides of the column were the flank riders. At the tail end were the drag riders. These youngsters riding tail were shouting hoarsely and riding in the cloud of dust kicked up by the great herd of cattle. They all had their ropes down, and tied securely to the end of each rope was a tin can containing a few large pebbles. These cans were whipped over the backs of the lazy or limping drag steers, and, along with much shouting, encouraged the stubborn cattle to travel faster.

We arrived quite early at the grazing grounds, and there was the usual excitement of changing horses. The foreman organized evening and night guards. Many of the riders wanted time off to go into town and do a little celebrating. Some wanted a few free hours to go to the movies. These unusual arrangements meant long hours for some of the ranch-hands who were too easygoing to refuse a friend who wanted time off. In the late afternoon and evening of this day, Saturday, the town folk from Swift Current drove out with horses and buggies and Model T Fords to watch

*Cy Thornton, Matador wagon boss (left), and Legs Lair, manager of the Canadian division of the Matador. Both of these men were Texans and were in the cattle business all of their lives. The photo was taken at the Gas Springs roundup in 1921.* Author Photo

the spectacle of such a great herd of milling cattle and the frantic riding of the cowhands who were trying to keep control of them. The curious crowd completely encircled the cattle except on the westerly side.

Between about five o'clock on Saturday afternoon and Sunday at about the same time, the discipline in herd control completely broke down. At times there were only one or two riders on the west. Early Sunday morning the cattle became impossible to hold, and I ran the horse herd in with the steers. Circling, I came upon only one other rider.

Who was at fault for the lack of organization is hard to say. Barton and his Ray Knight outfit were certainly reliable. All during this time no one gave me instructions or asked any questions. I don't know what happened to our own crew bosses, but it is almost certain that they had been excused from duty for that period.

At about five o'clock that Sunday Jim Reynolds appeared, and soon after, Cy Thornton and the rest of our cowhands showed up. Jim arrived on horseback. He asked me to run the remuda into the rope corral as he wished to catch a horse for the young Royal Canadian Mounted Police officer who was with him, and who was to escort us as far south as the Montana border. Where they all came from suddenly, I do not know.

Jim caught a little Colorado pony named Cottonpicker. Cotton was gentle, well-broke, and black as night. Jim used one of the Matador stock saddles out of the wagon for the young police officer. I remember it had a good-sized seat, pummel, horn, and cantle. The stirrups were relaced for the young man's long legs in order to make him comfortable while riding.

Reynolds gave the officer a boost into the saddle, and, to everyone's surprise, Cotton rolled his gentle black eyes and sailed skyward. Evidently, the Colorado pony decided that his United States citizenship meant he did not have to serve the Canadian lawman. After a little arguing far above the ground, the officer took command, and Cotton submitted quite peaceably to being ridden.

Our young RCMP officer proved to be a man of considerable talents and was of immeasurable assistance to us on the drive from Swift Current to Montana. We would often have to snake back and forth rather than travel a straight line as there were several areas of good, cultivated farm land on the way to the border. In some areas our scout had to select a winding trail that took us miles off course. Once or twice we were hemmed in by sparse, early growing crops and had to make our way across them. It was at these times that we were especially grateful for the young officer's diplomatic skills in settling damage claims right on the spot.

Farm and ranch dogs near our path were often a problem. Most often these troublemakers were first spotted by our scout, who called on the police officer for help. Once, a large stray farm dog in the ranch area we were crossing had to be destroyed by the Mountie. Before doing so he of course requested permission from the nearest rancher. With the officer's help, the cost of renting private overnight grazing was most often settled quickly and amicably.

Breaking camp early that Monday morning and moving out on the trail from the chaotic situation at Swift Current had been as sudden as the appearance of the Matador crew on Sunday afternoon. My guess is that Mr. Lair had come up from the Matador headquarters on the river and been very vexed with what he saw. He undoubtedly used strong methods to get his outfit moved from Swift Current at once.

The wagon horses were hooked up. The cook, Hayes, had not yet recovered from too much celebrating, but he was shoved up on his spring seat and given the driving reins. Johnnie and Button were cut loose and swung to the left, pulling the chuck wagon over the cribbing on a bored twenty-four-inch water well. The wagon tore the cribbing and windlass to ground level, but fortunately no horses were injured.

We only travelled five or six miles south to camp on Swift Current Creek. I had not had my clothes off on Saturday or Sunday night. Needless to say, my memory of that Sunday evening is very dim.

By early afternoon the cattle drive reached the south end of Lac Pelletier. Here there was quiet and good grazing. In 1921 the Lac Pelletier Valley was a green, peaceful place, and our long stay there allowed the cattle to get some much-needed rest. Just as important, it cleared the minds of some of the cowhands who had indulged in too much celebrating the night before.

I shall always remember Lac Pelletier for the one little dogie who died that night on the south shores of the lake.

On the morning of 27 May 1921 our trail drive wandered south toward the town of Cadillac, which was situated in a valley. From the higher ground to the northwest, we could see the tops of the grain elevators as we came about a mile from the town. From here our scout turned us abruptly to the southwest so that we would avoid crossing cultivated farmland.

On the evening of 28 May we camped in the northeast outside corner of a large pasture. The corner was about 2,000 acres and had water on it. There was good fence on the south and west sides, so herding day and night was easy.

It turned out that the huge pasture was the northeast corner of the old 76 cattle ranch. This ranch was owned at that time by Gordon, Ironsides, and Fairs, Limited. By 1921 the 76 ranch was much smaller than it had been at one time. Not too many years before this—probably even in 1910—the 76 lease encompassed land to the very outskirts of Swift Current and west as far as Maple Creek and well into the Cypress Hills. At one time it had reached as far south as the Montana border.

By prearrangement the 76 had cleared a portion of its range so that we could trail our cattle across the ranch. We were three days crossing the 76 from north to south. The first day from the north we came into the deep valley of the White Mud (Frenchman) River. We grazed the stock all the next day and rested on good grass and plenty of water.

It was here on this supposed day of rest that Barton's young nephew, Pistol, nearly got himself in deep trouble with an outlaw stampede bronc.

One of the Ray Knight harness horses was a big, strong, black gelding that was usually drawn in professional stampedes or rodeo finals in saddle-bronc riding. At one time, this horse was gentle and well broken, but for some unknown reason went loco when saddled. He had a reputation of being impossible to ride. The horse, called Powder River, had been bred and raised in the Alberta foothills.

Pistol was obsessed with the idea of riding Powder. His uncle, Barton, knew this and had forbidden Pistol to go near the horse.

This day, while all of the riders were up in the hills hazing the grazing cattle, Pistol, who was the night hawk, drove the remuda into the corral and caught Powder. The horse was gentle to handle and harness, but when saddled and mounted it was a different story. I was the horse wrangler and was there all of the time. I felt awfully uneasy about what was happening.

Powder stood quietly as Pistol got him ready to ride and carefully swung into the saddle. He tried to get Powder to step forward, but, being held up, the big horse stepped backwards instead, then sideways into a big looped breeching that was standing loop up on the ground. The breeching swung upward into Powder's flanks and all hell broke loose.

The seventeen-year-old was a pathetic sight. His face turned ashen-yellow, and he even dropped his riding reins and pulled leather with both hands. The big black simply went crazy and roared like a mad bull. I too became frightened but had enough presence of mind to quickly mount Blackbird and try and pick up my young friend and his loco horse. Powder would run for a hundred yards then suddenly duck his head and go in four different directions at once. All the while he never ceased bellowing. When I finally caught Pistol and snubbed Powder close on my saddle, the young man climbed over the rump on Blackbird, landed on unsteady legs, and started to throw up.

Almost at this moment Barton appeared. Getting off his horse he listened to Pistol's side of the story. Putting his arm around his nephew's shoulders, he told the young man everything was all right just as long as he wasn't hurt.

These are my last memories of Pistol and his uncle,* whose Ray Knight outfit had fulfilled its contract on the White Mud. From here they returned directly west to their home base at High River.

* Just before the last shipment of beef went out of Wiseton, and the Canadian Matador closed for good, we received word that Barton and his horse had drowned in some small river in Alberta. It was late in the season, and unusual for a river to be in flood at that time of year. That is the last and only word we ever had about Barton, the cattleman who never gave his first name.

# Montana At Last

Jim Reynolds was born in the big ranching country of Oklahoma where his parents were pioneers. He could not remember when he first sat a horse or roped his first calf; he had worked as a cowhand since he was a boy. In those early years, cattle were always worked from wagon camps on open ranges.

Jim ranched and worked cattle all of his life except for a period during the First World War when he drove pack mules in the U.S. Cavalry in France. These mules, which Jim led, were carrying large machine guns and ammunition right into the front-line trenches. Many of his mules were shot down around him. Jim always joked that the reason he was never hit was that he was so thin.

Reynolds was about thirty-five years old in 1920. It was difficult to judge his age as the wind and outdoor living had prematurely aged his face. These wrinkles gave Jim smiling eyes and a rugged handsome face.

Jim took me under his wing from the time I started riding for the Matador. It seemed I was always near him on the big cattle roundups. When I was the horse wrangler, Jim got into the rope corral with me to rope fresh horses for the riders. He showed me how to throw an overhand small loop that was best used when on foot in a crowded corral.

Reynolds was a good person, well mannered, with a rancher's principles of old-fashioned honesty. He knew all of the facets of cattle ranching and could tell at a glance the approximate age of a beef; its weight, and whether it was ready for market. He could heel or head rope, brand and doctor cattle on the open range. All of this made Jim Reynolds a top hand.

Of all the men working at the Matador, Jim was the one most often invited to nearby family-owned ranches for a social evening. In the hills to the north, there was a family with several attractive daughters, and one of these girls had taken dead aim on Jim.

I kept a pair of blue serge pants between the soogans in the mattresses of my bedroll. Sleeping on the pants night after night gave them a permanent crease as sharp as a razor. I also had a Scotch plaid woollen shirt, which had been purchased at Jack Wood's ranch store in Swift Current.

I always knew in advance when Jim was going courting. First I would hear him whistling softly after

*Jim Reynolds, pictured here at the roundup at Gas Springs, was top hand for the Canadian Matador. Tough, lean, honest, and an experienced cowhand, Reynolds had ridden the range from lower Texas to Canada.* Author Photo

returning from whatever work he had been doing that day. He would have a shave, and if we were camped at Bootjack Tank, he had a quick swim in the dam. Jim had his own devious ways of asking if he could borrow my pants and shirt, and it always came about that he rode a-courting on his fanciest horse and wearing my best clothes.

Jim would not return to camp until just before daybreak the next morning, as we were having breakfast. There was just time enough for him to change horses and eat before another day in the saddle.

It's amazing what a pretty face and the charms of a woman can do to an otherwise sensible man.

On our cattle drive to Montana, Jim was our scout and rode far in front, sometimes several days ahead, to explore the unfamiliar prairies for the best trail. He looked for water and good grazing so we could camp every twelve or fifteen miles.

In early June of 1921, although our destination on the Milk River was to the southwest, our scout found that we had to follow the small valley of Cottonwood Creek southeast to take advantage of its grazing and water. The higher ground on the stony Boundary Plateau was almost devoid of grass, and there was no water. After a day of travelling along Cottonwood Creek, we took a course southwest heading directly for Harlem. Reynolds and Cy Thornton decided that since water would be scarce on the remaining sixty miles or so of our trail drive, we had best cover every mile possible each day even if it meant spending some nights in a dry camp.

We crossed several creeks with some grazing and a little water, but at these places we stopped to rest for brief periods only. After two days and nights of almost continuous travel, we arrived at a large earthen dam. The reservoir formed by the dam was fed by big springs coming out of the stony moraine. The overflow from the dam created many acres of good irrigated grazing, and we rested the stock here for a day. For twenty-four hours the tired cattle ate, drank, bedded down, and chewed their cuds.

Meantime, our wagons were unloaded and repacked. The bedrolls were taken apart and aired, and minor repairs were made on broken equipment. After we had attended to these urgent chores, several of us rode to the top of the ridge of hills to the south to see what lay beyond. From this vantage point we had a panoramic view of the Milk River Valley below.

Reynolds, who had already been into Harlem scouting several days before, said that our destination and the end of our cattle drive was about fifteen miles away. He estimated that by tomorrow we would turn our steers loose in the holding pasture where they would be taken over by the Montana Matador in the Belknap Indian Reservation.

Our wagons were camped on level ground near large cottonwood trees and the river. The rope corral was stretched, and, except for a couple of horses staked nearby, the remuda was in a small fenced area near the holding pasture for the cattle. We were at the end of our drive, and were tired and exceedingly dirty. We all needed shaves and a good bath, and some of our clothes were pretty shoddy.

The morning after our arrival Cy Thornton said that he had our paycheques in his saddlebag. Mr. Lair had given them to Cy before we left Swift Current. Cy proposed that we all go over to the small Farmers and Ranchers State Bank in Harlem to cash our cheques. These cheques, by the way, were always drawn on the Matador Bank in Denver, Colorado, and were in U.S. funds, which at that time were at a premium of about twenty percent or more in Canadian dollars. I cannot remember what an experienced cowhand was paid each month but it was likely sixty or seventy dollars in U.S. funds.

Cy had not made any prior arrangements with the Harlem bank. It was not necessary since the bank already handled the Montana ranch's business. So we, eight or ten of us—whiskers, dirt, and all—saddled up and rode over to the bank in this small hamlet a couple of miles northwest on the railroad. Arriving there, we tied our horses to the hitching rail, then clanked and stomped, with spurs rattling, across the boardwalk into the front entrance of the bank.

The customers' entrance room had only one window, near the front door. A door from this room led into the back offices, and next, on the same wall, was a wicket similar to the old, country post offices.

Our noisy arrival caused a young lady to pop her head out of the wicket, and what she saw nearly made her faint. Her distress caused the young cashier-manager to pop up beside her.

We had all been living and working together so long that it seems we had become accustomed to one another's tough looks. However, it took Cy a long time to persuade the frightened manager that we were there for peaceful purposes, that we would give him Matador cheques in exchange for cash, and that this was not a holdup.

Our trip to the bank must have made our foreman realize that his Canadian Matador wagon crew looked like banditos or bank robbers. At any rate, after spending some time by himself in a far corner of the tent musing over book figures, he suggested that there was enough spare expense money to take most of the crew to the big town of Havre, fifty miles west of Harlem. We could go relax, and have shaves, haircuts, and a good bath. Cy checked on the passenger train schedules to see what could be arranged, and before the day was over everything was decided. We would leave on an early morning train from Harlem and return from Havre at 4 A.M. the following morning. The travelling distance was so short that this plan would give us almost a full twenty-four hours in the big town, even long enough to get our laundry done.

Havre, Montana, was a pleasant, busy little city— more like an overgrown western cowtown. It was a railroad divisional point where trains were made up and the crews assembled. The railroad had a large engine repair shop here so there was quite a colony of railroaders who were good local citizens. There were several fine hotels and many excellent eating places, mostly catering to ranchers and cowhands. Among the several moving picture theatres and places of entertainment, the most unique was The Honky Tonk. It can best be described as identical to the TV saloon run by Miss Kitty in *Gunsmoke*.

On arrival in Havre in the early hours of the morning, we checked into the hotel nearest the railway station. Cy got two large adjoining double bedrooms with baths. As we were checking in, the clerk, who knew the needs of a tough-looking crew such as we were, told us of the barber shop, bath house, and laundry next door. He directed us to a ranch store where work clothing was reasonably priced. Much of our clothing was so worn, dirty, and torn that it was not worth washing. As soon as the store opened we shopped for shirts, underwear, socks, and such. Good summer cotton work shirts could be purchased for one dollar or less.

Next was the barbershop called The Emporium. There we were boiled in steam, cooked until well done under hot towels, and scraped with razors until there was not much left of the original. Restorative shaving lotions and hair tonics were applied so that when we staggered out of the barbershop we did not smell like our old selves at all, but rather more like escaped polecats.

The desk clerk at the hotel was quite excited about the new troop of cancan dancers that had just been billed into The Honky Tonk. He suggested that we have our noon lunch there when it opened and remain as long as we wished since there was a continuous performance on stage until 2 A.M.

The Honky Tonk building was dark except for the stage at one end and the kitchen and bar with its shiny glasses, bottles, and huge mirrors at the other end. There were many four-place tables and chairs on the main floor as well as some private open booths along one side. The large room had a high ceiling, and it seemed that the whole place was unfinished and unpainted lumber.

We had just started our meal when the cancan showgirls came on stage. Someone said this was a repeat appearance and I could believe it—perhaps their thirtieth annual. It was hard to decide as they kicked high, showing their black garters, whether the view was best from the south or sunny side or from the north side in the shade.

When we arrived back in Harlem the next morning at about five-thirty, a couple of the fellows who had not gone to Havre with us were at the station with our saddle horses. Back in camp, on the bank of the Milk River, Jim Hayes had his usual delicious breakfast ready. After a couple of hours of good rest on top of our bedrolls in the shade of the cottonwood trees, we started repacking our wagons for an early start home in the morning.

We began our trail drive on 18 May 1921 at Gas Springs in the north Matador summer pasture. We swam the broad Saskatchewan River and crossed the U.S.–Canadian border, arriving at the end of our cattle drive in Harlem on the Milk River within a day or two of 12 June 1921. Every steer that we started with at Gas Springs was delivered in good shape to our colleagues in the Belknap Indian Reservation except for the one little dogie who died on the shores of Lac Pelletier near Swift Current.

We had been on the trail for twenty-five days, and the distance of our wandering course was about 350 miles, which made the average distance covered each day fourteen miles. It had been an unforgettable experience, especially for this young cowpoke, but, like the others, I looked forward to returning home and once again riding in our friendly Coteau Hills.

# Jim Hayes Feels His Oats

In May or June of 1920, Mr. Lair, manager of the Matador, was taking one of his bimonthly trips into Swift Current with his new Dodge touring car "to get her shod," as he always said. He took Earl, Jim Hayes, and me along. We planned to stay overnight, see a picture show, and probably do a little shopping at Jack Wood's Mens and Ranch Store. Jack sold those good Justin, special-made-to-measure riding boots, also Levi pants, with lots of rivets, and great pure woollen Scottish plaid shirts, also genuine Stetsons.

Earl and I registered at one of the finest hotels in town—the Heely. As it turned out later, so had Hayes. After the show, Earl and I had a late lunch at the restaurant run by Buster Wa and his folks on Central. It was very late by the time we returned to our hotel and went to bed. After several hours we were awakened by a dickens of a racket in the hall, which was crowded with guests and police. We found that the source of the ruckus was Jim Hayes and two very friendly ladies, in a room just a few doors down.

It appears that the ladies were not friendly enough, or that Jim simply wanted to show them who was boss. Wielding a chair, he chased one of the women under the bed. He then jumped on the bed, bringing himself, the mattress, and all down on top of the poor woman. She obviously felt that the risks of her profession had become too hazardous and protested with loud and piercing screams.

Jim noticed the other woman standing in the corner of the room next to the third-storey window. At the moment the police broke into the room, he was about to finish her off by throwing a chair at her.

Earl and I snuck back into our room as the officers led Jim to the paddy wagon. His language left little doubt that he had a very low opinion of the police.

Early the next morning, the sun shone through our window and the birds began to sing. In the distance, we heard the mellow notes of a trumpet, then more musical instruments of the Salvation Army—that blessed organization—joined in, blending into beautiful marching hymns. Soon the whole Army, coming closer now, broke into robust marching songs.

Earl and I looked down, and there—marching along in the front row—was our cook, Stetson in hand, among the most repentant of the sinners.

As Earl and I were checking out at the front desk in the hotel lobby, Hayes and the Salvation Army officer came in. He was freshly shaved and cleaned, and explained that the Army officer was to be his guest in the hotel coffee shop. We told him, after introductions, that we had not had breakfast either. At that moment, Mr. Lair came in to eat, so there were five of us at the table. Even though Jim did not say so, Earl and I suspected that once again the Salvation Army had somehow gotten him out of jail without charges being laid.

Cocaine, or snow as it was commonly called, was easily obtained without prescription in those early years. Persons with extreme changes in their personalities, or highs or deep lows, or extreme depression were often suspected of being addicts and were called "snowbirds."

Hayes finally broke the miles of deep silence as we drove back to the Matador by saying meekly, "Sorry for making such a fool of myself." There were no replies, but we all knew how terrible this confused man felt.

Hayes was recognized as the best line camp, or wagon, cook in the hills. His mastery of a five-gallon sourdough crock was legendary. Neighbouring ranchers, riding across our range, always managed to arrive at mealtime to get a good load of grub.

Once, when the cowhands were returning in the early afternoon to Red Shack Camp, they found Hayes on the roof, preaching to an imaginary congregation. But down below on the rough table, there was a wonderful hot meal waiting for them.

Hayes, with his swarthy skin, always claimed that he was the son of an East Indian princess and that his father was a high-ranking British army officer. If he returned to England, he swore he would inherit a substantial fortune.

One day, in the midst of the Matador drive, I saw another side of Jim Hayes. On a quiet afternoon I decided to ask him if he would like me to get up on the spring seat beside him and have a visit. He seemed delighted and stopped the outfit.

As I tied my saddle horse, Badger, to the hames on Old Shannon, little did I realize what was in store for me. In the next hour, sitting beside our cook high on the chuck wagon, this young cowpuncher was treated to a most intellectual lecture on geography and geology.

Hayes explained that the Matador's Saskatchewan ranch was within the great treeless, grassy plain of the Palliser Triangle. He told of that great explorer being commissioned to assess the area that is now Western Canada to determine its potential for farming and ranching.

During the time Hayes was talking, he spoke quietly and earnestly just as a private tutor would to his pupil. Perhaps the situation reminded him of his past, except he would have been the student rather than the private tutor.

When the Matador closed, Hayes lost the stability that Mr. Lair, our kindly manager, provided for him. However, when the community pasture was organized by the Saskatchewan government in 1923, under the capable management of the Perrin family, he worked once again for a kindly employer, and was able to return to cooking in his beloved hills.

*Chuck-wagon tent set up on a trail drive on the Canadian Matador.* **Courtesy the Perrin Family**

# Part Four
# So Long

# The Comfort Of the Coteaus

The instant Frankie Goodwin, the ferry-man, dropped the guard chain, the saddle stock of the Matador thundered over the plank flooring and apron of the big scow at the Saskatchewan Landing river crossing. We were almost home. The big hollow ferry reverberated to the pounding of many horses' hooves, sounding like a hundred Indian war drums.

The ferry had already crossed twice from the south. The horses and wagons from these trips were raising dust by now, well on their way to the home pasture six miles east. The horses in this third load seemed to fear being left behind, and they raced in and out of the many arroyos, or dry washes, with reckless speed. As they ran, with flying manes and tails, some whinnied like lost colts trying to find their mothers.

It was warm and dry, and there were all kinds of prairie whirlwinds or "dust devils" flying about. These small tornados carried into the swirling air even more dust, dry grass, and tumbleweed than we stirred up, and this hung suspended for miles along our trail.

Finally we came to the big wash. It was deep, wide, and steep-sided. We entered from the west side on a slope in the wall, then turned left or north and followed the bottom for a hundred yards to a small sloping escape at the eastern side. It took a dextrous teamster to negotiate his outfit through this maze. Faithful Old Shannon, on the pole of the chuck wagon, lumbered along at his fastest gallop. Jim Hayes had to hold the wagon's smoking brakes on continuously. Somehow he managed to escape without a wreck.

I caught up to the wagons just as they disappeared over the cutbank and into the arroyo. Below, I saw a single big work horse hitched to a buggy. Sitting in the buggy was a young woman and two small children. As I watched, the chuck wagon flew by on one side of them and the bed wagon on the other side. I had witnessed a miracle.

Dismounting beside the buggy and looking up, I could see that the young lady sheltering the two little chickens under her wing thought, "And now this horrible villain has come to assault me." I tried to comfort her in my most gallant manner by bowing low, sweeping my Stetson to the ground, and saying, "Can I help you, Miss?" With her hat askew and her eyes flashing disdain and fear, she replied coldly, "No, thank you."

A more practical solution was required than my first approach.

The lazy old work mare was cramping the wheels and about to upset the buggy. I straightened the harness and one shaft, which was over the old girl's neck. I felt my actions had somehow restored some of my lost respect. Nonetheless, I retreated quickly to the east, hiding my embarrassment in the swirling dust. I discovered later that the pretty little Miss with the two children was the eighteen-year-old school marm

*The river ferry at the Saskatchewan Landing crossing, 1917.*
Author Photo

from a nearby country school.

Our tent was sheltered on the west by a dense grove of trees. To the northeast, the high plank rails of the dip-vat corral gave protection from the wind. Our camping grounds were flat. On the river side, just a few steps away, was a bushy cutbank, through which the cook had a path where he brought our camp water from the river. It was down this path and in the river that we did our laundry. In our wanderings over a vast prairie since early spring, it was the nearest to being our home. The cattle drive to Montana and back was quickly forgotten in the comfort of familiar and friendly surroundings. Here, we were content.

Fluffy white clouds drifted slowly from horizon to horizon. I had found a perfect spot to lie on my back and gaze at the sky. My nest was lined with a generous cushion of prairie wool. All of this, and with my hat shading my eyes, created the perfect state for blissful dozing.

For long moments my mind was a complete blank. Once in a while I was conscious of Old Star, whom I had tethered to a nearby rock with my lariat, grazing quietly on the succulent grass. The metallic clink of his curb bit was the only sound to break the silence.

To save grass, early this morning, I had taken our horse herd to the school section just outside our pasture on the flats above the river valley to graze. I had received instructions to hold the horses on pasture until they wanted to return to the river to drink.

Meantime, all our crew except Archie Hawes and me were spending long hours under the supervision of a hard-driving carpenter foreman, repairing the large corrals, dip-vat tanks, and heating equipment.

Archie, riding the rough string, had eight or ten green broncs in his latest class, and these had to be worked on continuously.

For me the hardest job was staying awake.

Lying on my back and almost asleep, my attention was suddenly caught by a small brown speck flying almost among the clouds. Then there were two specks. Suddenly one of the specks folded its wings and plummeted toward the earth, dropping so fast it seemed it would never stop in time. Then slowly its wings unfolded and it shot upward. I was fascinated by this air show. For a time the birds sailed and soared and soared and sailed, hardly ever flapping their wings. Gradually they came closer and closer and I could see how large they were. I thought the brown birds were large hawks of a type I had never seen before. Much later, I learnt that they were golden eagles.

Golden eagles, during the height of falconry, were used by Kirghiz Tatars to capture antelope. In Europe, during the same period, they were flown only by kings.

For a week, as I grazed the horses on the school section, I was entertained by their magnificence. I looked forward each day to their return and speculated as to where their nests or eyries might be found.*

About half a mile to the north was a small homesteader's shack. Mounting Old Star, I rode there, and was greeted at the door by a young man. When I asked for a drink of water, he graciously invited me in. His home was one of those ten-by-twelve tarpaper shacks built of rough spruce lumber. The exterior was tarpaper strapped with laths. This shack was the successor to the old sod homes.

I drank heartily from a common dipper, which was in a pail of warm water sitting on a small homemade table. There was a bed, cookstove, and a cabinet made from an apple box. On this sat a wash basin and soap. Hand and dish towels were hanging on nails on the walls and did not look too sanitary.

When the young homesteader—he must have been lonely—asked if I was hungry, I realized that indeed I was.

When I looked at his cooking equipment, I noticed

---

*Years later, my good friend Ted Perrin provided me with further information about the eagles in this area. Ted is a hard-working rancher whose ranch buildings nestle comfortably south of Beechy near the Saskatchewan River and east of the old Matador dugout pasture. Besides ranching, Ted is a naturalist by practice and desire.

Ted told me that when he was a young boy, living with his parents in the buildings of the old Matador headquarters, after the ranch land had been turned into a community pasture, there were two eagle nests just a couple of miles north and west in what was known as the farm coulee. One nest was in an old cottonwood tree and the other high on a cliff. Sticks and brush were added each year. The nest was an immense affair by the time the venturesome youth climbed the tree to inspect.

When he dropped down the cliff by a rope, there was a nearly full-grown chick in the nest. It was still in its down and pinfeather coat. This young eagle was almost three feet tall and at close range looked like a formidable adversary. In the nest were the remains of a jack rabbit. There was also a fat duck whose feathers had been plucked as if by a human hand, and made ready for the oven.

broken egg shells stacked up behind the stove. Deep fat, from previous use, remained in the frying pan atop the stove. My host seemed pleased when I accepted his offer to eat. He made a quick fire in the stove and in no time at all I had wolfed down four eggs consumed with old fat and many eggshells, and several slices of dry bread with no butter. This, along with a couple of cups of quickly made tea, was one of the most enjoyable meals I had ever eaten.

As I thanked my new friend, he asked me with sincerity to come again. This I promised to do.

I rode toward the remuda and did not look back until I had gone a few hundred yards. When I turned to wave, I saw the young homesteader standing on the mound of earth that was his doorstep. He looked so forlorn and lonely.

I could foresee years of hard work and many setbacks before his good gumbo homestead of 160 acres would become a waving field of golden wheat. Who knows, perhaps this awkward boy would go to the school dance some time soon and be smitten by the pretty little teacher. They would dance, fall in love, marry, have many children, and live happily ever after.

And so it was in the olden pioneer days of the settling of the prairie west.

# All in a Day's Work

From where I was watering the horses in the river, I could hear the high, penetrating voice of Legs Lair as he scolded the carpenter foreman. Apparently Legs was upset about some of the planks the carpenter had replaced in the dip-vat corral.

Our kindly manager had noticed sharp corners and exposed edges in many places, and was asking that these be rasped or planed smooth and round. He had also observed that several "slivery" fir planks had been used and was giving instructions that these rails be replaced with spruce.

All the wagon crew, except Archie Hawes and me, had been working for several days to repair and rebuild our large dip-vat corral, tanks, and heating equipment. Mr. Lair was explaining in a rather firm manner why this work must be done correctly. Riding closer, I could hear him saying that when the stockyards were crowded, cattle could be injured by the exposed sharp ends and edges of improperly finished rails.

It was a weary-looking bunch of cowpunchers who were being worked to exhaustion by their hard-driving carpenter foreman. Most of the wagon crew were sleeping in the bunkhouse at headquarters. Hayes, the cook, had moved there too.

To add to our troubles, we soon learnt that the place was infested with body lice. What a lousy bunch of cowpunchers we were! There was no time for a good rubdown in kerosene, so we slept lousy, and endured our bedtime companions.

None of these bowlegged cowhands were accustomed to working on foot. After twelve hours of continuous standing or walking, their high-heeled Justin riding boots were causing sprains, blisters, and corns. Apparently it was easier to ride a tough mustang than a saw horse. It was sad to see such noble men reduced to sawing and scratching, both at the same time. Cy Thornton set a good example for his crew by showing it was almost possible to scratch, saw a plank, and smoke all at once.

The Matadors, wherever they were, always planned carefully before they built. First, the local manager suggested the location and made a rough design of the corral. He submitted this to the Denver office for approval. One of the head office officials then inspected the proposed site and assessed the need for such a corral. From there, the plan went over the desk of Mr. Mackenzie, the general manager. He, in turn, sent the drawings to the board of directors in Scotland, and explained why it was necessary to build the pens. If the plans were approved, an architect drew up the final blueprints, and Denver was given authorization to requisition the material and to call for a bid from contractors to erect the structure.

Dip-vat corrals were especially tricky to build. They required special pens, funnelling chutes, and sliding gates to control the cattle as they moved through.

At the dip-vat exit, there was a cleated, sloping ramp that started from the bottom of the vat and ended in a small dripping pen, which had a floor made of planks. The excess of the very warm sulphur and

*The cattle here are swimming through the dip-vat, which contains a mixture of lime and sulphur, to eradicate mange.* Courtesy Glenbow-Alberta Institute/ NB (H)–16–466.

lime solution drained back into the vat from the dripping pen. As the cattle swam across the dip-vat, which was about fifty-five to sixty feet long, men along the side of the tank used inverted shepherds' staffs to ensure that the cattle were completely submerged.

The purpose of dipping (immersing) the cattle in the vat was to eradicate a parasitic disease called mange, which, if untreated, would cause a great loss of weight in the livestock. The growth in cattle, particularly, would be retarded by as much as 150 to 200 pounds by marketing time.

The solution in the dip-vat was made of water, sulphur, and live lime. Its strength depended on the limit to which the sulphur and lime could be held in suspension.

The dip-vat was below ground level. Above ground and beside the vat was a square, fifty-barrel, wooden tank, where the solution was mixed. Beside the tank was a steam boiler that heated the solution to 110 to 115 degrees Fahrenheit.

The cattle were held in a small pen and worked from above and from the side with prod poles. From here they would run down a chute that gradually became narrower, thinking they could escape. But the chute led to a floor overlaid with a long sloping iron plate. Once they reached this plate they could not stop. Some of the animals tried but merely slid slowly into the tank. Other steers, seeing the vat just beneath them, took spectacular swan dives. Of course, the solution splashed high, but was not wasted due to the high wings built above each side of the vat.

There were two sliding gates in the chute. One was just at the point where the chute ended. When too many cattle were swimming in the vat, this gate was closed. The other gate was located where the chute first began to narrow. When the first gate was closed, the second one prevented too many animals from piling up in the chute.

While I was riding for the Matador, it was my job to operate the sliding gate at the foot of the chute and to see that cattle flowed through properly. Often, too many were in the tank at one time, and more were on the way. I would have to slide the gate across the chute quickly, often right in the face of some big, white-faced steer.

The Matador cattle were descendants of those wild Texas longhorns crossed for decades with Hereford bulls imported by the thousands from Great Britain in the early years. To all appearances, the stock I worked was typically Hereford, but in spite of many years of crossbreeding, and even though all the young stock were dehorned, some of the offspring still carried those long horns and were wild.

When we spotted a steer with horns, we had to have them removed. One of the fellows at the beginning of the chute would shout, "horns." As the steer was going by, my partner on the other side of the chute and I would snub the steer's head to the side rail and saw off his horns. Pine tar was applied to the area where the horns had been.

Although we operated under very dangerous conditions, there were very few accidents. Cattle, horses, and men suffered the odd broken bone but little else. In the two years I helped dip Matador stock, only one steer broke its leg. This was noticed in the drain pen. Pails of water washed down the sulphur and lime and he was butchered right there and then.

Under more ordinary circumstances, butchering happened like this: A young steer was selected and driven to our foreman, Cy, who hid behind a bush or rock with his rifle. The animal was dressed right where it fell. No saws were used in cutting up the meat, only knives and an axe, so the cuts of beef were those not usually recognized by a butcher.

But accidents on the ranch were inevitable, and there were many close calls. If one of the saddle horses fell frequently, without a good reason, he was put with the condemned saddle stock to rest. Once, when I was following the remuda to the river, the horses were very thirsty, and the entire herd was racing. I was riding a small blue roan pony called Donor, and we were almost flying in an attempt to catch up to the herd. Although the river flat was level, with no stones or badger or gopher holes, Donor fell suddenly. All I remember is lying on my back as Donor rolled over me; the cantle of the saddle just missed my face. When the horse got to his feet, he was as dazed as I was. This is just one of the simple things that could have resulted in a serious accident.

Another time, Jim Reynolds was roping a big steer to be doctored for what we called "cancer eye." The lariat, which was tied to the saddle horn, broke. The popping of the breaking rope nearly tore off a finger on Jim's right hand.

There were, of course, more serious accidents. One winter, before I rode for the Matador, a ranch-hand by the name of Smith was hauling hay to headquarters. He had twelve to fifteen miles to haul hay with a four-horse team and rack, which could carry about two tons. Late one night Cy became worried about Smith when he did not return at the usual time. When Cy rode out to see what had happened, he found Smith under the load of hay with his feet sticking up through the bottom of the overturned rack. Cy tore the wooden rack apart with his hands, unloaded some of the hay, and, with the superhuman strength an emergency provides, pulled Smith out from under the rack. The young man was almost frozen solid.

The pole team was down and had been cut to pieces by the sharp-shod lead team. No doubt they had to be destroyed by Thornton.

Smith died a few minutes after Cy pulled him out. Even so, the foreman took off his heavy outer clothing and covered the body before he rode back to headquarters for help.

Accidents aside, those of us on the payroll of the Matador led a happy life. This was in contrast to the situation on several other large American ranches, where morale could sink fairly low. The rule of the pistol and hired gun was just a decade in the past. In fact, it was on a chilly December morning in 1909 at Le Beau, South Dakota, that Murdo Mackenzie's son Dode was shot in cold blood by a drunken hired gun in the Phil Dew Fran Saloon. The killer, a supposed friend, returned Dode's smile as the younger Mackenzie approached with an outstretched hand. Without warning, Bud Stephens shot Murdo Mackenzie's favourite son once in the chest, and as he turned in surprise Stephens pumped two more bullets into his back. Dode Mackenzie, at this time, was manager of the South Dakota Matadors. At his trial the killer pleaded self-defence and was declared innocent by a bribed or intimidated jury.

Dode Mackenzie did not even go for his gun when he was shot. The young man had a great circle of friends, no known enemies, and was never quarrelsome. Perhaps a rival group carrying guns believed that in killing Dode they would somehow intimidate Murdo Mackenzie, or frighten him into quitting his job as general manager of the Matadors. Little did they know this grand old stubborn Scot.

There were many lighter, more humorous moments at the Matador as well. Mr. Lair, under the terms of our lease with the Canadian government, was to do some experimental farming. There was a coulee with a small plot of level ground close to headquarters, and, each year, Mr. Lair took the whole wagon crew to this spot, where a four-horse discer was always left. Old Shannon and two big unbroken broncs were hitched to the discer. A lariat was thrown around the neck of the outside horses and then snubbed to the saddle on a couple of outriders. Why Mr. Lair had taken me and several others along is hard to understand. He probably wanted to prove that a horse really could be trained to pull a farm implement.

Horses also proved useful in other unexpected ways. The Matador had its own large vegetable garden. Vegetables that would keep were stored in a root cellar for continuous use throughout the year. The whole crew was assembled when it was time to plant the garden. The horsepower came from Johnnie and Button, who were hitched to what most ranchers thought of as the devil's instrument—a one-furrow walking plough. It was a circus. One cowhand drove the team, another—usually dumb and strong—took the "handlebars." Legs Lair was shouting to the ploughmen to go this way—no, that way. The rest of us, including the cooks, were spectators.

It was a joy working for the Matador under the leadership of Legs Lair. From this incredibly honest, outspoken old man flowed wisdom and a desire for excellence, mixed with humour and kindliness.

When the sweet corn from the garden ripened in the fall, Mr. Lair called in all the riders, no matter where they were, and staged a grand corn feed. The cooks took the day off as Legs put on an apron and did all the cooking.

A couple of nights before the big feed, Legs set out some night lines in the river to catch fish. With the corn there were always huge platters of pike, pickerel, and the occasional goldeye.

When Mr. Lair had finished loading the long table in the dining room with plates of food, he asked us to be seated. When we were all in our places, only then did he remove his hat, wipe his hands on his apron, and sit down at the head of the table. Then, with bowed head, he gave thanks for the food he had prepared.

We felt humble in the presence of this grand old man. The body of this six-foot, six-inch gentle Texan was large, and his bones carried the soul and spirit of a giant.

# Minding the Ranch

Cy Thornton had ridden to the Matador headquarters, about twenty miles southwest on the Saskatchewan, to get the mail. When he arrived back at the Basin Springs wagon camp, he had a message for me from Mr. Lair. Legs wanted me at the ranch buildings to look after the barnyard stock for a couple of weeks. The Saskatchewan ranch was moving to the Pine Ridge Indian Reservation in the Black Hills, and Mr. Lair had been offered the position of manager of the South Dakota division. But he could not decide if he should accept. Our bookkeeper, R.G. Reid (called "The Scotchman" by Mr. Lair), had already been transferred to South Dakota.

We were camped at Basin Springs—in the most northeasterly township of the Matador ranch—to check watering holes and ride fence. The spring got its name from the bowl-shaped plain in which it was located. The plain was about five miles across and surrounded by high hills, with a small gap to the southwest. In wet years, ponds provided the basin with water. But in dry years, the big spring, flowing continuously out of the high sloping walls on the eastern side of the south Coteau Hills, could be depended upon to supply many cattle with water all through the year.

The spring was about a third of the way up the gentle slope. There was no draw or great crevice at the mouth of the spring, but because of the small area around the spring it was necessary to build considerable defences so that the ground would not be trampled into mud by the cattle. Just below the gushing spring was a tublike structure built from pilings of planks, secured firmly at their base by large rocks and stones. From this tank a sluice released the water at a sharp downward slope into a huge wooden watering trough. This rested on a firm foundation of stones. The ground around the watering tank was paved with flat rocks. The entire structure, including the area around and above the spring, was enclosed in a sturdy fence, except the watering tank from where the cattle drank.

I never did find out who built the facilities around the spring. They included an exquisite water wheel that some artistic unknown had constructed and placed in the sluice. Here it sat on its frail axles turning endlessly, as though it had been doing so forever.

It was a mid-August morning when I left for the ranch buildings. The sun was peeking over the eastern horizon trying to decide what kind of day it would create. The soft caressing breeze felt promising, and there was just the right amount of cloud cover.

I was riding Blackbird as we headed south, possibly a little to the west of the hay flats. Cruising in

*Jacob Rouse, a man few people knew well, is shown here breaking Matador land with oxen.* **Courtesy Perrin Family**

second gear, over a sea of prairie grass, Blackbird's speed allowed only brief glimpses of the remains of the hay stacks that had been built by the mysterious Jacob Rouse. One of these spots was likely the place where Smith had been crushed and frozen to death.

Jacob Rouse was an unusual person. Whether you were in Great Falls, Lethbridge, Calgary, the Cypress Hills, or Swift Current, you would hear people talking about this man. But, talking aside, no one really knew him. Jacob Rouse was an enigma.

Rouse had freighted to or from all of the above places at one time or another, sometimes with oxen, or with horses or mules on a jerkline. The twenty animals were strung out one after the other and were hitched to many wagons. Rouse was very likely the inspiration behind the painting *The Wagon Boss* by famous Montana cowboy painter Charles M. Russell. When freighting was no longer profitable, Rouse ploughed the prairie with one of those ancient many-furrow tractor ploughs pulled by twenty oxen. He drove these teams by himself.

For a number of years, Jacob contracted to cut hay for the Matador. He did so with the help of only a couple of Indian men and half a dozen mules. The mowing was done with two mule mowers, and the gathering of the hay with two mule hay rakes. Then the hay was stacked with a bucking pole.

I saw Jacob Rouse only once, in the summer of 1920, when he was visiting Mr. Lair. Rouse looked unkempt and seemed rather talkative for the recluse he was rumoured to be. His feet had been so badly frozen at one time that he had to have them amputated, except for the heels and ankles. He stumped around in homemade heavy leather shoes and had only a trifle of a swagger. The adventures of this prairie character would fill several books.

Shifting into overdrive, Blackbird started floating over the cushion of prairie wool. Horizons came and were gone as the single-footed pace of Blackbird made each mile seem short. He spurned the prairie sod with a fast tattoo of flying hooves, and his speed defied gravity. Riding Blackbird gave one many mood changes. This was most noticeable when we were riding down the hay coulee, with its swerving turns. Going down from the high country on these trails and turning gracefully left then right was like dancing to the music of a Strauss waltz.

It was typical of Mr. Lair to meet us at the first gate into the home pasture. Also there to greet us was his pack of ever-present wolf hounds. When we asked Legs how he knew when to expect us, he said his puppies had told him.

As we were walking from the first gate to the buildings, leading our horses, Mr. Lair betrayed his excitement about the trip to South Dakota. He asked me to look after a number of things for him while he was gone. I was to take especially good care of his puppies. Looking down, I could see, walking protectively between the boss and me, the battle-scarred leader of the pack. This old gladiator, the killer, had survived many savage life-or-death battles with prairie wolves. As I looked down at him, it was easy to see from his chewed-up, fang-scarred face that he was fully capable of looking after himself. But no matter, he was still a little puppy to Legs.

The only hands at headquarters were the farm handyman, the cook, and Mr. Lair. I was to see that the six or eight cows were milked and their calves properly cared for. Legs took me on a tour of inspection. All the animals had names. One little fat calf he called "Tightwad." I questioned him about the name and he said, "Oh, that one. That's because he's a little constipated."

Finally, Legs put his saddle in his new Dodge touring car and was off to the Black Hills. His puppies missed him most. He had left his leather jacket, which he normally carried everywhere, behind at the ranch. It was spread in the shade outside near his office window. When the hounds were near it, they seemed perfectly content.

Before Murdo Mackenzie would accept the position as the North American general manager of the Matadors, he had insisted there be three policies laid down and that he be given authority to enforce these rules ruthlessly, if necessary. The policies would apply to all employees no matter what their position. They were:

1. No card playing on Matador property, by anyone, any place or any time.
2. No liquor. Absolutely none on any of the Matadors.
3. No cattle could be owned or raised by any of its employees.

To prevent the making of home brew, orders were given to all Matador purchasing agents that they were not to procure fruit of any kind that could be used to make intoxicants. Raisins were specifically mentioned.

Neither the farm handyman, Dave, nor I knew

of these rules, and it seemed the cook was not aware that raisins were a no-no, either, for he had a large stock of them. When I got the key to the commissary from the cook, I was pleased to be able to help myself to handfuls of the forbidden fruit.

Dave and I borrowed a large earthen crock from the cook. We crushed gallons of chokecherries that grew in clusters just behind the cow barn, put them in the crock with five pounds of raisins, five pounds of sugar, some water, and one yeast cake. We covered the brew with a white cloth and shoved it under one of the beds in the common bedroom.

The cook, who knew nothing about our brewing, discovered the smelly, frothy mixture about a week later. He was a little huffy about it at first, but refrained from throwing the grog away. He must have been secretly wondering what the effects would be if he took just a wee nip or two.

He found out. Just before supper one night, as Dave and I were milking the cows, we heard a lonesome off-key howl coming from the kitchen. We hurriedly turned the calves loose on the cows to finish the milking and rushed to the house. There sat the cook, singing, nearly overcome with admiration for his new-found talents. The magical effects of our brew contributed, no doubt, to this self-adoration.

Dave and I decided we had best finish our chores, so we strained the milk through a cotton cloth into the cream-rising pails before experimenting with the potent brew ourselves. These pails had taps at the bottom from where the skim milk could be drained off, leaving only the thick good cream behind. There was a viewing glass built into the bottom of the pail so that you could tell when all the skim milk had been drained. The cream would rise to the top in one of these pails when left standing overnight. The thick cream was used at the table in coffee, on fruit, and for butter-making. While fresh, some of the skim milk went to the calves. The rest made cottage cheese or yoghurt. Nothing was wasted.

We rose before daybreak every morning, and by breakfast we had fed the stock, milked the cows, and called the horses in for feeding by pounding on a pail.

Our sleeping quarters were much improved from when we had been here repairing the corral. The lice had left the bunkhouse and our bodies on the second or third day, when our clothes had become infused with the sulphur and lime fumes. However, lice were much easier to sleep with than sulphur and lime. A sore chest and smarting eyes meant we could hardly breathe, much less sleep. Any metal we carried—belt buckles, bachelor buttons, coins—had turned black.

During Mr. Lair's absence we had a lot of time on our hands. This gave us an opportunity to look into every building and place of interest on the headquarters compound.

Our first visit was to the house, with its kitchen and large dining room on the east side of a central hall. On the west side of the hall was a common bedroom in which were several beds. On the south end was a door leading into Mr. Lair's combination bedroom, office, and parlourlike room with its bay windows. From here you could look out over the pasture and toward the river. Mr. Lair's quarters ran across the full width of the house. The office of the bookkeeper was here also.

On Mr. Lair's bed was a large fur robe made from prairie wolf hides, which were the trophies of many long and savage battles of his hounds. One corner of the room was reserved for his favourite and fastest hound. This greyhoundlike animal slept on a couch near Mr. Lair's bed. Legs talked to this speedy character as he would to a person, and had named him "Sonny."

The compound contained the commissary, blacksmith shop, bunkhouse, large horse barn with hayloft and lean-to, and also the cow barn. There was a well near the kitchen door; it was from here that the cook rang the triangle to summon everyone to eat. There was another shallow well and a watering trough near the barn corral. To ensure that no gate was left open, you had to step up and down over a stair when you went to or from the house and horse barn.

The musty root cellar, with its many bins for storing vegetables over the winter, was an intriguing place. You entered by stairs that went down into an antechamber, lifting and closing a trap door as you went. An inner, frost-proof door admitted you into the root cellar proper. The light from a kerosene lantern revealed a dank, gloomy underground room with a high ceiling in which the temperature never became too warm or too cold.

The whole place was a mass of cobwebs and fungus. When we blew out the lantern to leave, we were in total darkness. Searching for the inner door and lifting the hatch to daylight, one had the feeling of barely escaping the clutches of an angry ghost.

Although old enough to do a man's work, we were obviously young enough to fear the dark.

# The Old Man Returns

By 11 A.M., there was an ominous, depressing feeling in the air. The farm animals seemed to sense impending trouble. It was hot and still, unusually so for this early in the day. The cows and their calves stayed close to the barns as if looking for shelter from something that would come out of the blistering haze to the west.

By one o'clock the western sky displayed a formation of storm clouds. Here in the compound of the Matador ranch headquarters, in the shelter of the Saskatchewan valley, the heat was stifling. We were trapped in a hot vacuum with not even the slightest breeze to relieve us. The wolf hounds were lying nervously in the shade of the house, tongues out, panting. They whined restlessly.

By three o'clock, thick black clouds had totally obscured the sun, and we found ourselves in a weird world of half darkness. To the south, in the western sky, a funnel cloud appeared, spiralling eastward. Almost directly west, where the clouds were most dense, a grey streak shifted constantly, indicating hail.

At first, as the storm gathered, we did not hear the rumble of thunder in the distance. But before we knew it there were flashes of lightning, and all too soon we heard the thunder bouncing off the hills of the river valley to the west.

Suddenly, in this dreamland of semi-darkness, the quiet was shattered by a crash of thunder that shook the ground and a magnificent bolt of lightning. Then more and more thunder and lightning jarred the earth. The front of the storm was here. Tornadolike winds swept the ground of anything that was light and loose and carried it high into the air. A great wall of water and hail descended upon us. In half an hour, we received more rain than had fallen all year.

Suddenly, it was as if a giant tap had been turned off. The rain ceased. In an instant the sun was shining brightly, and the air, which had been hot before the rain, now felt cool and refreshing. The prairie rainstorm had rolled over us violently, and now its terrifying winds, lightning, and thunder echoed and reechoed in the river gorge as it retreated to the east into the canyons of Seven- and Nine-mile coulees.

The little brown hen and her twelve new chicks came out of the small box shelter Legs had made for a nest. The little hen pecked at drops of water on the blades of grass and scratched the ground to uncover seeds for their first meal of the day.

The rain was still dripping from the roof when

*Legs Lair (left) and his beloved hounds. The man on the right is likely local rancher Robert Cruikshank.*
Courtesy Perrin Family

Mr. Lair arrived home from his trip to South Dakota. He had been gone for one month—one week longer than he had planned.

We were pleased to see him. Our pleasure, however, was not to be compared to that of his hounds. The big goofs ran around like delighted little fox terriers. They jumped on him, whined, and ran in circles to get the old man's attention. There were a lot of childish goings-on, and it was not until after supper that we were able to hear about the trip.

The yellow light of a small kerosene lamp lit the room as Mr. Lair related the story of his trip to the Black Hills. His usual high, loud voice was now a soft southern drawl and only rose in pitch when he was emphasizing something of special interest. The three hounds were lying quietly on the floor. The only interruption came when the big killer whined softly in his sleep and jerked and trembled. In his dreams, he was probably defending himself against a pack of wolves.

Legs had arrived at the Pine Ridge Indian agent's office at the peak of a heated argument between Reid (Legs's former bookkeeper) and a local man about the distance to some place nearby. Anyone of good manners would have accepted the local man's word concerning how far it was to this place, but not the know-it-all Scotchman. The Scots on the payroll of the Matadors were usually in office or administrative positions, and the Texans, who had spent a lifetime in the saddle and living with cattle, often did not fully accept them.

After long discussions with many people at the Pine Ridge Indian Reservation and nearby ranches, Legs discovered that a large number of cattle on their ranges had been disappearing. Similar disappearances of Matador stock had also occurred in the Belknap Indian Reservation at Harlem, Montana. To Legs, this represented great management problems.

He found, too, that cattle did not finish to nearly the same weight on Black Hills grass as those in Montana or Saskatchewan. As four-year-olds, the steers and spayed heifers were about 150 pounds lighter than those finished on most other northern ranges. There was an apparent shortage of some vital minerals in Dakota soils.

The extra week Legs was away was due to an invitation he had received to the Cattlemen's Association meeting in Denver. He said he never heard so many windy speeches about nothing in all his life. Neither was he impressed with the closing banquet at a grand hotel. Most of the guests, and even some of the waiters, were dressed in "monkey suits." He said standing around so darn long before eating was sure hard on the corns.

All the guests lined up as they were admitted into the banquet hall and went past a large glass tank that contained live mountain trout. Legs explained that a chef dressed in white, with a high hat, dipped out the trout you pointed to, and, supposedly, prepared it just for you.

Legs complained that the big fish he had selected did not resemble the little sardine that appeared on his plate. He said he felt like asking for his money back.

It was confirmed in Denver that the Matador wanted Mr. Lair to continue his association with the company in the capacity of manager of the South Dakota division. But they were in no hurry for his decision. Legs thought the financial rewards of the company's offer were ample, but he wondered, at his age, if he should take on a new career that might include problems with the Indians.

The yellow flame in the kerosene lamp was feebly trying to stay awake. It had burned almost all the midnight oil as the tale of the old man's trip to South Dakota unfolded.

Suddenly Legs asked me what I would think about going to Brazil to work for a ranching company in South America. The question startled me, even though the subject had been a topic of discussion by the ranch-hands for several months.

While in Denver, Legs had been approached by an official of a Paris and New York empirelike ranching company who explained that his company wanted several young, North American-trained cattlemen to work for them. He was particularly interested in employing those who had more than an elementary education. Legs said the pay scale was excellent and the prospects for advancement good.

The old man said if I decided to work for The Brazil Land, Cattle, and Packing Company, at its head office in São Paulo, my first duty would be to accompany a shipload of Hereford bulls from Great Britain to Brazil. The boat was to leave Great Britain just after Christmas to arrive in South America in that country's early summer. All of this would fit in with the shipping of our last beef herd from Wiseton in late November or early December. These steers were going by boat to Great Britain and would arrive there before the departure of the bulls to Brazil. There was no need for a quick answer.

I will always wonder how life would have turned out had I taken them up on their offer.

# Tough Broncs And Tall Tales

I can remember when there were cowpokes better known for their storytelling than their ability to ride a tough bronc or their skills with a fifty-foot lariat.

These masters of juggling the truth practised their art best in the eerie darkness, usually just before all hands had drifted off to sleep. A simple question evoked the telling of a marvellous and, of course, true story. This telling was enhanced by a cold north wind howling through the knots and chinks of a drafty bunkhouse.

The question this night was, "What range raised that big handsome sorrel gelding, Red Top?" This brought a sleepy but quick response from one of those best known for telling tall tales.

His story went like this: Red Top was the colt of a little Arabian mare who escaped her owner in Wyoming—or was it Colorado?—into big canyon country and was captured into the harem of a big vicious wild stallion.

"At birth," the teller swears, "the wild sire drove off a mountain lion that would have killed the helpless colt before it could rise to its feet."

Red Top was a common topic of conversation. He was in the rough string of Archie Hawes in the years 1920 and 1921 and likely as a green bronc in 1919 when Byklum, who used to have Archie Hawes's job, was breaking horses for the Matador.

Red Top was a golden sorrel, a beautiful gelding. He had the appearance of a perfect saddle horse, and looked as though he would be gentle and easy to break. These were only impressions. The reality was that Red Top was a vicious, incorrigible wild animal, whose beautiful appearance and smooth-flowing action seduced Archie Hawes into believing that he could become a wonderful saddle horse.

Whenever Archie roped Red Top in a corral, and snubbed him to a post with dallies, the horse would fight the rope until he choked himself down. He would then strike out with his forefeet, like a tiger, and kick like lightning, snorting all the while as if trying to spit in Archie's face.

Usually, the first night Archie was working a horse, he would tether him to a heavy log on a fifty-foot lariat. By morning you found a very tired, subdued pony, with quite a few rope burns and a little hide missing, but well broken to tether. But not Red Top—no matter how many nights he spent with lariat and log.

Archie Hawes was a professional horse trainer. He was a graduate of the world famous Barry Horse Train-

*In addition to telling tall tales, these Matador cowboys amused themselves by sharpening their wrangling skills. The cowboy with the lariat is "spinning rope."*
Courtesy Perrin Family

ing College, led by Professor Barry in Iowa. The Barry methods of breaking or training a horse, as practised by Hawes, often brought unbelievable results. Balky horses in harness could be made to pull, and vicious, biting broncs would become gentle and good working animals.

Archie was always in the process of breaking eight or ten broncs. These were in various stages of being tamed. As they became saddle and bridle wise, docile and submissive, they were turned over to the cowhands. It's surprising how quickly they became useful in working cattle.

Archie kept his methods a secret. He took the horse to be trained behind the barn or behind a big bluff of trees. He carried a buggy whip, and someone suggested that the horses were brought into submission with this.

If the whip was used, it would have been lightly, for Archie was fond of horses and not at all cruel. Some thought he used a war bridle made from a lariat. This was not so, as there was never any blood from the nose or mouth of the horses Archie tamed.

When Archie and Red Top appeared from behind the bluff at the dip vat, Red Top was following Archie like a devoted dog. When he stopped in front of us, Archie gave a slight jerk on the lariat around Red Top's neck. The horse rose on his hind legs and took a step or two. Archie then dropped the lead rope and crawled under the belly of this very wild animal.

Archie, now lying on his back under the horse, took one of Red Top's hind legs and held it above his face. Throughout all of this, the animal seemed mesmerized.

The time had come to bridle and saddle Red Top. The horse stood quietly as Archie performed these tasks. He mounted slowly and had seated himself nicely in the saddle when, as happened so many times before, Red Top simply ran away, almost out of the country, with Archie.

Archie had used a severe long-shanked curb bit with the chin strap buckled snug, but no matter how hard he pulled on the reins, it had no effect on this cold-jawed runaway horse. This was Archie's last attempt to tame this loco bronc, but Red Top's legend continued to enliven the tales told around prairie campfires for years to come.

# Rustlers On the Range

The Jennings and their many relatives were cattle rustlers. Most of the cattle they rustled came out of the Coteau and White Bear hills, and a few from Bone Pile Ridge and the 3 Bar ranges. The Jennings's permanent camp was in the big coulee six miles straight south of the present village of Hughton, in the northeast corner of the White Bear Hills. The dugout dwelling, barns, and corrals were southwest, just a few turns into this coulee and were well hidden.

During the years 1903 to 1910 Matador stock ranged from the Saskatchewan River to as far north as the present towns of Rosetown and Milden, an area of over seventy miles, north to south. From 1910 to 1915 they could be found grazing throughout the Coteau Hills. It was inevitable that the Matador would lose many cattle to rustlers. Management staff of the Matador and other ranches were aware of the problem and subsidized the hiring of plain-clothes and Royal North-West Mounted Police, and later Saskatchewan Provincial Police, to ride the hills.

In August 1921, when our wagon was at the Basin Springs camp, I rode into the new town of Beechy with Cy Thornton. Cy wanted to see Jim Gallon, the Saskatchewan Provincial Police officer who was in charge of the detachment there. We noticed as we rode into town that the railway grade had been completed to Beechy, but the steel had not yet been laid. Two grain elevators were in the process of being built. One was almost finished and already painted. The big sign on it showed that it was owned by the Nerby Elevator Company. There were a few shacks on the streets that had been staked into lots and there were numerous lumber piles, indicating that the new town already showed promise of being a thriving business centre.

I did not go with Cy into Jim Gallon's office-shack, but laid on a lumber pile across the street. I fell into a deep sleep and did not awaken until Cy shook me. It was pitch black as we rode back to the wagon. There was little conversation during our ride home, but it was obvious that Constable Gallon and Cy had discussed cattle rustling for many hours.

In the sparsely settled country of those early pioneer years, getting fresh meat delivered was a problem. There were beef wagons operating as private businesses. There were also cooperatives called "beef rings," which served great areas of the country. The democrat wagons they used were pulled by two horses. They had large, well-ventilated boxes with doors at the back that kept the meat quite fresh and free from flies.

*Unlike their American counterparts, Canadian cowboys were not allowed to carry guns as Cy (Tom) Thornton (middle) and his friends did when this photo was taken in Texas. When in Canada, Cy usually hid a derringer in his pocket. The gun went off accidentally in 1922, shooting Cy in the leg.* Courtesy Opal Bradford

The operator of these outfits had a weekly circuit and was expected to be at specific locations at a particular day and hour. This circuit included regular visits to homesteaders, stopping places, inland stores, and so forth. One week's work included a circle of about 150 miles and the handling of many quarters of beef.

Some of these meat-wagon operators were the outlets for the Jennings's rustled beef. It appears that the Jennings always delivered the butchered beef at some safe location to those retailers who were gang members.

I knew five local meat retailers very well. Four of them bought their live beef and did their own butchering. Joe Lalonde and Paul Royer had a modern slaughter house on their ranch near the village of Lacadena. Ole Nygaard ranched and farmed at Saltburn between Lacadena and the hamlet of Sanctuary. There was a French butcher in the village of Plato—his name I do not remember. He did his own buying and had his own slaughter house. The fifth was Jack Smith, a member of the Jennings gang. He operated from the present-day town of Elrose (then known as Laberge).

In 1915 the police rounded up the Jennings gang. Jack Smith was found guilty of selling stolen beef and received a sentence of two years plus one day. He lost the Elrose shop and most of his other fairly substantial assets. As well, his wife left him while he was in jail. The ring leaders of the Jennings gang received stiff prison sentences. When they were discharged from jail, it is believed they returned to their home state of Kansas.

When Jack Smith got out of jail, he lived in his homestead shack south of Elrose. I went down with my wolf hounds and stayed with him for a week or so. Hunting was good, but Jack was very depressed and would not hunt with me. Finally, after seeing me come in with coyote hides every day, Jack saddled his big black, and the excitement of the chase helped to bring him out of his depression. However, I know that selling stolen Matador beef weighed heavily on his conscience.

Ole Nygaard, as well as operating a beef wagon, had a still out in the hills for making home-brew. He produced an excellent product that was much in demand, making this end of his business very profitable. The three merry French butchers, Joe Lalonde, Paul Royer, and the fellow from Plato were among his best customers.

One time these three lively butchers were on a joint

cattle-buying venture and had hitched one of their meat wagons to a wild team of broncs. They had all been imbibing Ole's best brew. The Plato butcher had nodded off, so Joe and Paul put him in the meat box to sleep it off. Just then they arrived at the ranch where they planned to buy some cattle.

The rancher appeared at the door as they drove up, so Joe shouted "whoa" and threw the driving reins aside. Joe and Paul jumped out of the rig leaving the wild team unattended. For a moment the horses stood still, but only for a moment. Joe and Paul said afterwards it was one of the prettiest runaways they had ever seen.

First the team tore through the barbed wire fence that surrounded the yard. Then they went across the road allowance and through the three-strand wire fence on the pasture opposite. The rig made several wild loops in the pasture, and when the horses made a quick swing to avoid hitting the fence on the way back, the wagon upset. The door on the meat box flew open, ejecting the Plato butcher.

When Paul was asked later whether the butcher had been hurt badly, he replied in his unique mixture of English and French that although there was a lot of blood on the Plato butcher's face, that face was such a mess already that no accident could possibly make it worse.

In 1916, Joe and Paul acquired an old Model T Ford chassis. They built it into a light truck with the meat box at the back. Paul generally ran the meat route, driving the Ford just as he would a team of horses. He often forgot how to stop. At these times, usually on a runway down some steep hill, he pulled hard on the steering wheel and shouted "whoa" in French. Although he upset the rig many times, he was never seriously injured.

One day he was driving over the top of Bone Pile Ridge, going west down into the Lacadena river flats. The road was little more than a few furrows on the township line and was not intended for wheeled traffic. The car embarked upon its out-of-control race at the lofty crest of the ridge.

This day Paul had traded a couple of beef steaks for a big live rooster. The rooster and Paul's ever-present cattle dog were on the seat beside him as the old Ford started to break speed records. One of the front wheels hit a large rock and the Model T did a grand somersault, landing upside-down on top of Paul, the rooster, and the dog. The impact killed the rooster and broke the dog's leg. The only effect it had on Paul was to release plenty of colourful French swearing. It must be grand to lead a charmed life!

Joe Lalonde and Paul Royer were good friends as well as business partners. Joe was married to a tidy, stout little French lady whose maiden name was Delisle. Joe was a big man, tall and dark, with a strong, clear baritone voice, which he readily used for singing.

Joe had many sides to his personality. He had complex capabilities for making money. When he did so, he spent lavishly on jewellery and clothing for his wife and himself.

Paul, on the other hand, was a small man, not very tidy, with heavy bones and enormous hands and feet for a man his size. In fist fights—and he had many when drinking—he broke the noses of a good number of big, tough men. Wise men did not challenge this little wildcat. Most amazing was that this rather rough-looking person was an accomplished classical pianist.

The West was peopled by all sorts of characters in those days. Like any other place, it had its share of rustlers and rogues, but the majority of the folks I knew were decent and honest men and women—people I was proud to call friends.

# Hanging Up The Saddle

The three wild horses stood on top of the high pinnacle in the southern Coteau Hills. One of the animals was dapple grey, one shiny black, and the third a brown bay with a blazed face and four white stockings. Over the years the three had proven impossible to break to saddle or harness. Likely the only reason they were being corralled now was to admire their beauty.

This was the second time Cy Thornton had sent Earl, Archie, and me to bring in these fast-running outlaws. They had eluded us the first day. We were all mounted on our best circle horses. Earl had his long-winded sorrel. I was on little Silver with his large black eyes and nostrils. Silver also had that big joint on his left front knee, but this did not stop him from running for miles and hours. Archie was on one of his newest broncs, which looked and handled as though he would stand up well on a long and fast circle.

At last it seemed as though we had our quarry where we could encircle and then drive them the thirteen or fourteen miles southwest into the dip-vat pasture. But they were ready for us. When we rode to the top of the pinnacle, the wild ones had disappeared as if by magic. We discovered they had circled around us and were now at our backs to the northeast.

Archie organized another plan that involved making a long circle east, then travelling north again and spreading out about a mile apart. I was riding

*Stan Graber, 1994. Photo taken in west central Saskatchewan. It was in this area that thousands of head of Matador cattle once roamed at will, and Stan, as a young man, learned to rope and ride.* Courtesy Peter Wilson of The StarPhoenix

the south swing, half a mile north of the straight eighteen-mile fence on the south side of the Matador summer pasture. From here we started our sweep west.

The ground ahead of me was not hilly, as it was farther north. Silver wanted to run, but I had to hold him back since that would have put us in front of the drive. It was exciting to watch Archie in the distant north as he leaned over his horse and rode at a reckless pace, barely managing to keep the outlaws from breaking back behind us once again.

The next time I saw the wild running horses was when they tried to get around Earl, close to my north. Earl's speedy sorrel was able to head the runaways toward me, and that's when Silver went into overdrive. Archie's scheme had worked. For ten miles, the wild ones tried to outrun us. They charged past the open gate into the dip-vat pasture, but Archie, anticipating this, had gained just enough ground to head them off and push them back through the gate.

Riding in an English steeple chase could not equal the excitement of that day. Following wolf hounds hunting coyotes is great sport, but running wild horses is the most thrilling of all.

The noon camp we set up later was on the top of a windy and winding ridge snaking north toward Wiseton. We unhitched the wagon horses and gave each a pail of water and fed them a gallon of oats in nose bags. We were fifteen miles north of the Matador basin gate on the second day of the drive to our shipping pens with the last of the Matador beef, a herd of 2,500.

During the last forty-eight hours of our roundup and trail drive, we had experienced some of the worst weather imaginable. At the beginning, we fought the milling cattle all night in a terrible blizzard. Then the high northwest wind turned cold, so cold it was difficult to drive the cattle against it. In reasonable weather we would have been at least one day's drive farther on the trail.

We unhitched the stove cart and set the stove on the ground. Hayes attached a section of pipe and lit a fire, thinking he could make us some hot food, but the best he could do was brew a pot of coffee. I remember making a jam and cheese sandwich. Although all of the ingredients were frozen, that sandwich tasted so good to a cold and hungry cowboy that strawberry jam and cheese sandwiches continue to be one of my favourites.

How we endured such hardships is difficult to

understand. Frost bites were taken as a matter of course, lack of sleep on a trail drive was accepted, and a cold bed on frozen ground was the only comfort for total exhaustion. Regardless, we loved the life and our work. The isolation of the range and the scarcity of visitors probably insulated us against the bugs of civilization.

It was after dusk on the second evening of our noon camp on the cold, windy hill when we drove the steers into the pens at Wiseton. The full moon had just come up, and as it rose higher in the sky it seemed like the middle of the day. The ground and all stationary things were enveloped in hoar frost.

It was still and cold, terribly cold on this mid-November night in 1921. Steam was rising from the hot cattle and horses in the many pens in the stockyards, as well as from the watering troughs in the big pens. Before our arrival, the railroad brought in a heated tank-car of water and had filled the troughs, and the feeding racks along the outside rails of the pens were full of hay. The cattle would be given four hours of rest and time to feed before we would commence loading the first train. Meantime, we would set up camp, get a hot fire going, and have a good meal and a short rest.

Once we started loading, it was not long before those of us who were working on foot with prod-poles in the small loading-chute pens shed our heavy outer clothing, in spite of the bitter cold. It was hot work and heavy clothing only slowed you down when confronted with a fast-charging steer—which was often—as they were being crowded together in the small pens.

After one train was loaded and had pulled out, there was a lapse of a couple of hours before the next one came in. While resting in the tent, waiting for the last train to arrive, Jim Reynolds asked me to come over to his bedroll. There he opened his war bag and showed me several relics that had been given to him in Paris when he was with the American troops during the German surrender in World War I. Among these relics were a silver knife, fork, and spoon, an American Army issue wool blanket, and a black lace shawl, which some grateful Parisian lady must have worn over her hair.

I knew Jim was a good friend, but until that moment when he said, "I want you to have these, Stan," I did not realize the extent of our friendship and how close he felt to me. When I accepted these truly precious gifts, I noticed that there was very little left in his war bag. The table silver and lace shawl have been lost over the seventy-odd years since I said "goodbye" to Jim, but I still have, and treasure, the American Army blanket.

This shipment of live beef to Great Britain by train and ship was to be the last from the Canadian Matador. We swept and combed the miles and miles of pasture of one of the largest ranches ever known in Canada and were very sure that no cattle had been left in the river breaks or the hills of this great old ranch. However, some apparently eluded us, for, in 1922, riders found 250 Matador steers in some isolated coulees.

Jim Reynolds was to accompany the cattle from Wiseton by train and ship right through to Great Britain. He had assistants, but he alone was responsible for overseeing the proper handling of the 2,500 steers to their destination.

The last car was loaded at about three or four in the morning by the light of the brightly shining moon and kerosene lanterns. My heavy clothing and other riding items such as chaps and spurs had been left in the space between the loading platform and the pens. It was too dark for me to notice that a steer had escaped just as it was going into the cattle car and had fallen into the enclosed space where my clothing was.

It all happened so quickly that no one was able to shout a warning until I was about to pick up my things. It was only a step to the high rails on the pens. Jumping high, I managed to reach the top rail and pull myself a little higher just as the big steer's head struck the planks between my outstretched legs.

The train pulled forward until the caboose was opposite Jim's gear. We passed his things to him slowly, as if somehow we could delay the departure of this good friend. As we were shaking hands, Jim suddenly noticed that he had on my Jack Wood's Scotch plaid shirt. He offered to take it off, but I suggested he return it when we met again next spring. Both of us knew how unlikely that was.

In my last talks with Jim it never occurred to me to ask if he might be going from Great Britain to work for The Brazil Land, Cattle, and Packing Company in South America. Nor did I think of asking what his plans were for the future. Most probably he came back from Great Britain to the friendly hills of his home state of Oklahoma. In any event, I have never had a letter from Jim nor any word about him since that night at the Wiseton stockyards.

Two lonely moaning blasts on the whistle of the big steam freight engine was the highball for the last

Matador cattle train to pull out. As the train started moving, we followed the caboose to the end of the loading platform. Our friend was on the back end of the train with a train-man's lantern, and as he gradually faded into the darkness of the east, he waved this, railroader style, indicating that all was well.

It was quiet now. The sounds of bawling cattle and men shouting as they loaded wild steers had faded into the night. Cy Thornton, relieved of the worry of the dangers to his crew, seemed quiet and pensive.

Cy had ranched and ridden the hills from Corpus Christi and San Antonio to two hundred miles north of the forty-ninth parallel, and in so doing had learned how to survive in harsh and primitive surroundings. He was a good wagon boss who never asked from his crew that which he would not do himself.

Cy would have realized that we came into Wiseton to ship this last load of cattle with a full wagon crew. Three men had gone with the trains, and I would be leaving for my home in Elrose in a day or so after we had cleaned up around the yards and our camping place at the stockyards. That would leave very few under his charge when he returned to the ranch.

The mournful sound of the whistle on the departing train had barely reached our ears when we realized how dead tired we were. Cy had arranged with the local hay haulers to fork off a good supply of hay to be placed under our bedrolls in the tent and over the frozen ground. It made a wonderfully soft cushion. A good meal, a red hot fire in the stove, and a snug tent ensured us a long and restful sleep. We knew that our responsibilities here had ended—there was no reason to rise early the next day.

Before I mounted the next morning, we casually shook hands, and, in an off-hand manner, said our goodbyes. I have seen none of those friends since.

As I started west to my home at Elrose, I was mounted on that tough little mustang Old Baldy, and leading my pack horse Bulldog. After riding a short distance I turned and waved to the Matador wagon crew. Little did I know in that wave, I was also saying goodbye to the life of a cowpuncher and that never again would I earn a living riding the Canadian prairies.

# A Parting Shot

In the early spring of 1966 a youngster made an unusual and exciting discovery as he was rummaging in the nuisance ground at Lucky Lake, Saskatchewan. He found, sealed in a tobacco can, the Last Will and Testament of James Bamet Henson (Swede), dated 28 September 1919.

Ironic humour, biting sarcasm, and a peek into a segment of Saskatchewan's history are all contained in the will made by this former ranch-hand of the Matador.

Henson's will was dated 28 September 1919. This was before the incident with Joe and Lightfoot that caused Swede's dismissal. It is obvious that he despised Mr. Lair even before the Matador manager fired him.

Bill Bullock, mentioned as an executor in the will, came to Canada with the Old Turkey Track outfit, an American group that ran a ranch in the Rush Lake area. He worked at the Matador until 1912, when he moved to the 6–T Ranch, which was owned by Robert Cruikshank of Moose Jaw. Bill was a rancher all his life, starting as a boy in Texas. For most of the time that he was employed by Mr. Cruikshank, Bill worked alone in a line camp. He was so cantankerous that Mr. Cruikshank could get no one to work with him.

Bill was a small man. When he was a child, he had lost one eye in a bow-and-arrow accident. He was tough—a good man with cattle—and looked after his boss's stock as though they were his own. He rode the range until he was eighty-four years old. After retiring he lived in a Salvation Army home in Saskatoon until his death at the age of 104.

So Long 117

I saw Mr. Cruikshank several times when he was visiting Mr. Lair at the Matador headquarters. He was handsome, distinguished looking, a good dresser, and articulate. It was obvious from the way Mr. Lair treated him that he valued this rancher's oinions.

From the content and composition of the will, it appears that Henson was an educated person. Where he came from and where he went to no one knows. His bones are likely buried with those of other pioneers on the lonely, lee side of some windy pinnacle in the Coteau Hills.

This is the Last Will and Testament of me, James Henson of the ranch of the Matador Land and Cattle Co. in the postal district of Saskatchewan Landing, made this 28th day of September in the year of our Lord one thousand nine hundred and nineteen.

I revoke all former wills or other testamentary dispositions by me at any time heretofore made, and declare that this only is to be and to contain my Last Will and Testament.

I direct all of my just debts, funeral, and testamentary expenses to be paid and satisfied by executors hereinafter named as soon as conveniently may be after my decease.

I give, devise, and bequeath all my real and personal estate of which I may die possessed in the manner following, that is to say: I direct my executors, William B. Bullock, of the 6-T Ranch, Herbert Alexander Knight, of the Hills, and Frank Dudley, formerly of the 3-3 Ranch, to immediately sell by public auction the whole of real estate situated in the City of Swift Current, Sask., and with the monies thus procured to create a fund, to be ultimately used for the extermination of that class of vermin, commonly known as farmers, who are at present polluting, by their presence, the country adjacent to the Saskatchewan River. I further direct my aforesaid executors to dispose of my horse, saddle, bridle, chaperajos, bed, and clothing, either by public auction or private sale, and to pay the proceeds of such sale to my sincere friend, Gladys Baker, as a slight remembrance of her many amiable qualities.

I bequeath to Loused Louis Thompson of Horse Butte one package of insect powder and one cake of Lifebuoy disinfecting soap in recognition of the fact that he is able to get dirtier, in a shorter space of time, than any person that it has been my lot to meet.

All the residue of my estate not hereintofore disposed of I give, devise, and bequeath unto Isidore Laplante of Saskatchewan Landing and High Point, P.O., and I nominate and appoint William Bullock, Herbert Alexander Knight, and Frank Dudley to be executors of this my Last Will and Testament.

I will and bequeath to J.R. Lair of the Matador Ranch one package of Rough on Rats, and one ounce of Kill 'em Quick Gopher Poison, and recommend that he take same immediately. I further direct my executors to annually donate two hind quarters of Matador beef to the person who poisoned the hounds of the above mentioned J.R. Lair in the month of December 1916, such beef to be procured during one of these frequent fits of temporary insanity, to which the mis-manager of the Matador ranch is subject.

This is a codicil to my Last Will and Testament bearing date the 28th of September, 1919, and which I direct to be taken as a part thereof. I give, devise and bequest to George Windsor my Navajo saddle blanket; to Pete Laplante my rifle; to William Vincent Smith my rope; in recognition of the fact that they are respectively the best rider, the best shot, and the best foot-roper in the hills. Finally, I leave to each and every Mossback my perpetual curse, as some reward to them for their labors in destroying the Open Range, by means of the most pernicious of all implements, the plow.

As witness, my hand this 9th day of May, 1922.
James Barnet Henson.

# Cow Country Dictionary

*Arroyo.* Spanish for a small steep-sided water course. Also known as a dry wash. Usually no water in it except during a flash flood.

*Bed wagon.* A companion to the chuck wagon. Sometimes called the "hoodlum wagon." Used to carry the bedrolls, extra supplies, and equipment when the pastures were being worked by the chuck-wagon crew.

*Bench.* A plateau.

*Blackleg.* A usually fatal disease of cattle, especially young cattle.

*Bluff.* A grove of small trees.

*Bottom.* Slang for staying power, endurance, in a horse.

*Broke.* As in a horse that is broken to ride or drive.

*Bronco.* Spanish for a wild, untamed horse.

*Buckboard.* A kind of heavy buggy without springs.

*Bull cook.* Assistant cook, the flunky.

*Bull Durham.* A kind of fine cigarette tobacco, sold in small bags and favoured by ranchers and cowhands.

*Butte.* Usually a high flat-topped hill with steep sides.

*Cavvy.* Spanish for a herd of loose, extra horses on a roundup. A remuda.

*Cayuse.* An Indian pony. A mustang.

*Chaps.* "Chaparreras." Spanish for leather or fur leggings used to protect a rider's legs.

*Cheek.* To grasp firmly the side of the bridle on your horse as you are mounting.

*Cold-jawed.* Used to describe a horse that seems oblivious to the bridle.

*Chuck.* Food or grub.

*Cinch.* "Cincha." Spanish for a saddle girth.

*Circle horses.* Fast, long-winded, high-strung horses used to round up cattle on big ranches.

*Concha.* Large, decorative silver button from one inch to two inches in diameter. Used on chaps, bridles, and leather riding equipment.

*Condemned horses.* Sick or blemished animals that are unable to be ridden.

*Corral.* Spanish for an enclosure, usually made of poles, to hold stock.

*Coulee.* "Couloir." French for a steep-sided gully or water course.

*Dally.* "Da la vuelta." Spanish. To make a dally is to give a twist of the lariat around the saddle horn.

*Dip vat.* A long, narrow tank where cattle are forced to swim through chemicals to eradicate the parasitic skin disease, mange.

*Dip-vat corral.* A large holding pen, usually made of poles, built near a dip vat.

*Dogie.* Slang for a young steer.

*Draw.* A shallow gully.

*Eveners.* A light beam of wood or metal, approximately four feet in length, with a hole at the centre. A pin is placed through the hole to fasten the eveners to the wagon. "Whiffletrees" are attached to the ends of the evener. This arrangement ensures that each horse pulls its proper (even) share of the load. Usually for two horses pulling a wagon.

*Felloes.* The wooden rim of a wagon or buggy wheel over which the iron tire is shrunk.

*Fetlock.* Joint of a horse's leg just above the hoof.

*Freeze-up.* The first time the ground freezes, usually in late fall.

*Glass eyes.* Also called "China eyes." Are of pale opaque blue, most often found in horses with a blazed face or in pintos.

*Goosy.* Ticklish. Trembles and shrinks away when touched.

*Haze.* To drive animals from horseback in order to turn them back or prevent them from going in the wrong direction.

*Heel flies.* Not flies, but the larvae that bore into the flesh of domesticated animals and emerge, on their backs, as warbles. In the fly stage they lay their eggs in the heels of cattle, driving them crazy in the hot days of late summer.

*High-tail.* A slang verb to indicate taking off in a hurry. Fleeing.

*Homesteader.* A settler who came west to take free land for farming.

*Horse skinner.* Driver of horses who often uses a bull whip too severely.

*Jingle.* A time at dusk or early dawn when the remuda or horse herd is being corralled. It is a quiet time and named for the tinkling of bells attached to some of the saddle horses.

*Lariat.* "La reata." Spanish for a rope or lasso used to catch horses and cattle.

*Latigo.* Spanish for a leather thong connecting the rigging on a saddle to the cinch.

*Loco.* Mad or crazy. Range animals became so from eating locoweed.

*Loose-herd.* Letting livestock graze, when being herded, without being bunched too closely.

*Makin's.* Enough Bull Durham tobacco and papers to make a cigarette.

*Maverick.* An unbranded animal.

*Nigh pole.* The right side of the pole of a wagon. A horse on this side is the "nigh horse."

*Night hawk.* The night herder or night wrangler of the saddle horses.

*Off pole.* The left side of the pole of a wagon. A horse on this side is the "off horse."

*Oil skin.* Raincoat made of waterproof material that kept the rider dry on a rainy day. Most often called a "slicker."

*Outfit.* Slang for most everything: a ranch, a chuck-wagon crew working the pastures, a camp, equipment. You name it.

*Outriders.* Men on saddle horses riding at the sides of a speeding chuck or bed wagon to guide it safely in the right direction.

*Pinnacle.* The highest hill overlooking those around it.

*Pinto.* Spanish for "spotted" or "painted." Most often it will be a horse with splashes of red and white spread across the body, with a blazed face, pink nose, and "glass eyes." It will usually have a white mane and tail and will be standing on pink hooves. Then there is the piebald; nature really got mixed up when she painted this little pony.

*Prairie wool.* Hay that clings together like wool. Is mostly a mixture of cured fescue and blue stem grass.

*Pull leather.* Grasping the saddle horn so as not to be thrown from a bucking horse. To some riders, it is considerably more honourable to be thrown from a bucking bronc than to pull leather.

*Ramrod.* A boss or wagon foreman. The "push."

*Remount string.* The six or eight saddle horses, in the remuda, assigned to each rider.

*Remuda.* Spanish. Same as "cavvy." Spare horses working with the chuck-wagon crew, usually a herd of 125 horses on the larger ranches.

*Ride clean.* To ride a bucking bronc without grasping the saddle to prevent being thrown. A classy and honourable way to ride a bucking horse.

*Riding fence.* Inspecting fences on horseback and repairing when necessary.

*Rig.* A wagon, buggy, democrat, or some other similar means of transportation.

*Road allowance.* Strips of land sixty-six feet wide and one mile apart, running north and south and east and west, reserved for or bordering a road.

*Rough string.* Young unbroken broncs, when they first came off the range, went into the rough string. The man who rode the rough string was experienced in handling wild horses. His job was to tame these broncs, making them good saddle horses with a lot of cow sense. There were usually five to ten horses in the rough string at one time.

*Running horses.* Riding a fast horse while trying to catch horses that have escaped and gone wild.

*Rustle.* Cattle or horses do this when they find grazing on their own, without human assistance, e.g., when they "winter out." Can also be what cattle or horse thieves do.

*Saddle horn.* A small iron post, above the forks, on the pummel of a stock saddle. Used by ropers, of cattle or horses, to dally or tie their rope to when an animal is caught.

*School section.* Sections 11 and 29, each of 640 acres, set aside in every township by the surveys for school purposes.

*Slip scraper.* A small, shovel-like scoop pulled by two horses. Used to move earth, and repair earthen dams, or "tanks," as they were called by Texans.

*Snub.* To tie onto or tie an animal to a post or saddle horn.

*Soogans.* A Scottish name for a down-filled comforter or blanket, used as a mattress, in the bedroll of a cowpuncher.

*Switcher.* A horse with the nervous habit of switching its tail as if being bothered by flies, while, at the same time, dancing on its hind legs when walking.

*Tie fast.* To tie your lariat or rope solidly to the saddle horn instead of the wraparound dallying where the end of the rope is held by hand.

*Wagon boss.* Foreman or boss of the roundup crew.

*Walleyes.* See *Glass eyes.*

*War bag.* A small canvas bag, with a draw string, in which riders carried their personal belongings. Such bags were used during World War I, hence the name. Also called a "turkey," the bag was kept in your bedroll when on the trail.

*Wash.* See *Arroyo.*

*Whiffletree.* A crossbar, pivoted at the middle, to which the tugs (traces) of a harness are fastened.

*Wintering out.* Livestock turned loose in late fall to rustle (find) their own food during the winter months.

*Wrangle.* To herd or work cattle or horses on a ranch.

*Wrangler.* A cowhand who, riding a saddle horse, herds and works cattle or horses.

# Stan Graber

Stan Graber was born on a horse and cattle ranch near the present town of Mohall, North Dakota, in 1902. A few years later his family moved to Saskatchewan, living first in an Irish colony near Muenster and then in Kindersley and Elrose. Stan got his first job at the age of ten, driving oxen on a farm near Smiley, Saskatchewan, breaking the prairie soil. At fifteen, he began working on the family cattle ranch. Like many children in that era, Stan could not attend school regularly because he had to work, but he managed to complete high school in Elrose.

As a teenager Stan worked for several ranches, becoming accustomed to the long hours and hard work that went along with life in the saddle. In 1920, at the age of eighteen, he went to work as a cowhand for the legendary Matador Ranch, north of Swift Current. He spent the summers of 1920 and 1921 there, participating in the last cattle drive from Saskatchewan to Montana when the Matador closed its Canadian operation.

Stan rode home on his trusty mount Baldy after that last drive. He had received an offer to work for the Matador Land and Cattle Company on its ranch in Brazil, but chose instead to work for the bank in Elrose. Stan's choice would lead eventually to a career in business, as he went on to become a Registered Industrial Accountant, a member of the Research Club of Chicago, and president of the Saskatoon chapter of the Cost Accountants Society. He worked for Bowman Brothers Ltd. in Saskatoon from 1935 to 1955, and was general manager of the Winnipeg firm Gillis and Warren Limited, a distributor of wholesale automotive products, from 1955 until his retirement in 1958.

Stan had met his future wife, Floss, when they were youngsters; the Baldwin and Graber families were pioneer neighbours and friends in Elrose. Floss and Stan were married in 1928. After Stan's retirement, they travelled extensively, visiting most of the North American continent in their Airstream trailer, and also travelling to Hawaii, Mexico, and the Caribbean.

Stan began his writing career in 1990, at the age of 88, when the popular prairie newspaper *Grainews* asked him to entertain their readers with his memories of the last cattle drive from the Matador. Stan went on to produce a regular column, which became the basis for his book *The Last Roundup*, and he continues to write for the paper.

Stan and Floss currently live in the seniors' residence, Luther Heights, overlooking the South Saskatchewan River in Saskatoon, where they enjoy an active retirement with their many friends and acquaintances. On 26 December 1994, they celebrated their sixty-sixth wedding anniversary.